The McCarthy Hearings

Jesse G. Cunningham, *Book Editor*
Laura K. Egendorf, *Assistant Book Editor*

Daniel Leone, *President*
Bonnie Szumski, *Publisher*
Scott Barbour, *Managing Editor*
Sandra Somers, *Series Editor*

 OPPOSING VIEWPOINTS® SERIES **AT ISSUE IN HISTORY**

GREENHAVEN
PRESS®

THOMSON
GALE

San Diego • Detroit • New York • San Francisco • Cleveland
New Haven, Conn. • Waterville, Maine • London • Munich

LIBRARY OF CONGRESS CATALOGING-IN-PUBLICATION DATA
The McCarthy hearings / Jesse G. Cunningham, book editor; Laura K. Egendorf, assistant book editor.
p. cm. — (At issue in history)
Includes bibliographical references and index.
ISBN 0-7377-1347-X (pbk. : alk. paper) — ISBN 0-7377-1346-1 (lib. : alk. paper)
1. Army-McCarthy Controversy, 1954. 2. United States—Politics and government—1945–1953. 3. United States—Politics and government—1953–1961. 4. Right and left (Political science). 5. McCarthy, Joseph, 1908–1957. I. Cunningham, Jesse G. II. Egendorf, Laura K. III. Series.
UB23 .M38 2003
973.921'092—dc21   2002069323

Printed in the United States of America

Contents

Chapter 1: Analyzing McCarthy's Methods

Chapter 2: Assessing McCarthy and McCarthyism

of the senator's fears were possibly realized, the stigma of McCarthyism led to an era of more liberal domestic and foreign policies.

Foreword

Historian Robert Weiss defines history simply as "a record and interpretation of past events." Both elements—record and interpretation—are necessary, Weiss argues.

> Names, dates, places, and events are the essence of history. But historical writing is not a compendium of facts. It consists of facts placed in a sequence to tell a connected story. A work of history is not merely a story, however. It also must analyze what happened and *why*—that is, it must interpret the past for the reader.

For example, the events of December 7, 1941, that led President Franklin D. Roosevelt to call it "a date which will live in infamy" are fairly well known and straightforward. A force of Japanese planes and submarines launched a torpedo and bombing attack on American military targets in Pearl Harbor, Hawaii. The surprise assault sank five battleships, disabled or sank fourteen additional ships, and left almost twenty-four hundred American soldiers and sailors dead. On the following day, the United States formally entered World War II when Congress declared war on Japan.

These facts and consequences were almost immediately communicated to the American people who heard reports about Pearl Harbor and President Roosevelt's response on the radio. All realized that this was an important and pivotal event in American and world history. Yet the news from Pearl Harbor raised many unanswered questions. Why did Japan decide to launch such an offensive? Why were the attackers so successful in catching America by surprise? What did the attack reveal about the two nations, their people, and their leadership? What were its causes, and what were its effects? Political leaders, academic historians, and students look to learn the basic facts of historical events and to read the intepretations of these events by many different sources, both primary and secondary, in order to develop a more complete picture of the event in a historical context.

In the case of Pearl Harbor, several important questions surrounding the event remain in dispute, most notably the role of President Roosevelt. Some historians have blamed his policies for deliberately provoking Japan to attack in order to propel America into World War II; a few have gone so far as to accuse him of knowing of the impending attack but not informing others. Other historians, examining the same event, have exonerated the president of such charges, arguing that the historical evidence does not support such a theory.

The Greenhaven At Issue in History series recognizes that many important historical events have been interpreted differently and in some cases remain shrouded in controversy. Each volume features a collection of articles that focus on a topic that has sparked controversy among eyewitnesses, contemporary observers, and historians. An introductory essay sets the stage for each topic by presenting background and context. Several chapters then examine different facets of the subject at hand with readings chosen for their diversity of opinion. Each selection is preceded by a summary of the author's main points and conclusions. A bibliography is included for those students interested in pursuing further research. An annotated table of contents and thorough index help readers to quickly locate material of interest. Taken together, the contents of each of the volumes in the Greenhaven At Issue in History series will help students become more discriminating and thoughtful readers of history.

Introduction

For nearly five years in mid-twentieth-century America, the most powerful figure in politics may not have been President Harry S. Truman or President Dwight D. Eisenhower but a previously little-known junior senator from Wisconsin. From the time of his speech in Wheeling, West Virginia, on February 9, 1950—when he claimed that 205 Communists were working in the State Department—until his peers in the Senate voted on December 2, 1954, to censure him, Joseph Raymond McCarthy enthralled and angered the nation with his accusations of Communist infiltration in the government. These accusations led to a series of public hearings that became known as the McCarthy hearings. McCarthy ultimately met his downfall when he took on the U.S. Army; the Army-McCarthy hearings, held in the spring of 1954, exposed the senator as a blowhard political opportunist.

It may seem surprising that McCarthy came to be somewhat of an American icon of the late 1940s and early 1950s. However, Joseph McCarthy was not the first person to express concern about the specter of communism in the highest levels of the federal government. The Cold War had been in full force for several years before his speech in West Virginia. What McCarthy did was capitalize on the nation's fear of communism that had become, for a time, epidemic. As scholar Margaret Mary Barrett explains in *American Social and Political Movements, 1945–2000*, "Characterized by excessive trials, antiradical legislation and anticommunist propaganda, McCarthyism was instigated by the fear of Soviet aggression. It was a paranoid reaction to Soviet advances in technology, espionage, and the political conversion of other nations in the postwar period. It was, in essence, a drastic domestic response to growing Soviet power."

The Origins of the Cold War

The United States and the Soviet Union, although allies during World War II, had a strained relationship. When the war ended, the two superpowers disagreed over the future of Poland, where Soviet leader Joseph Stalin had already established a pro-Communist government in 1944, following the Soviet troops' victory over Germany. At the July 1945 Potsdam Conference, the leaders of the United States, the Soviet Union, and Great Britain engaged in tense debate over the boundaries of newly conquered Germany, with the Soviets ultimately gaining the upper hand. The Soviet Union wasted little time taking control of Eastern Europe. Between 1944 and 1947, Communist governments were established in Albania, Yugoslavia, Romania, Bulgaria, Hungary, and Poland.

By 1947, the Cold War—the term coined to describe the military buildup and continual tension between the United States and the Soviet Union—had begun in earnest. Concerned that the Soviet Union would take over Greece and Turkey, which were both embroiled in conflicts with Communist forces, President Truman delivered a speech before Congress on March 12, 1947. In it, he laid the groundwork for what became known as the Truman Doctrine, stating that the United States must provide aid in order to ensure stable democracies throughout Western Europe. Ten days after the speech, Truman signed into law a $400 million aid package for the two nations, both of which ultimately withstood the Communist onslaught.

Fear of Communist Infiltration

While the Truman administration was developing a postwar foreign policy, others began to question whether Communists had infiltrated the highest reaches of American government. Some of that speculation was given validity much later, in 1995, when the American intelligence files known as the Venona Papers were declassified. Those files contained intercepts of Soviet spy cables and other materials revealing that Communist sympathizers had indeed infiltrated numerous government offices and agencies early in the Cold War. Amos Perlmutter, the late professor of foreign affairs at American University in Washington, D.C., writes that these sympathizers were prominent within Franklin D. Roosevelt's administration. According to Perlmutter, "From the mid 1930s through the mid 1940s, there were high-level Soviet sympathizers in the administration of Franklin D. Roosevelt, and . . . during World War II, the Soviets relied on many spies in sensitive spots to provide them with a wealth of military information, including early designs of the nuclear bomb."

In the late 1930s, the government began responding to the growing threat of communism. The House Un-American Activities Committee (HUAC) was created in 1938 to investigate suspicious individuals and subversive organizations. Probably the best known of the committee's early investigations was that of a man named Alger Hiss. In an August 1948 HUAC hearing, confessed ex-Communist Whittaker Chambers accused Hiss of having belonged to the Communist Party during the 1930s, when Hiss was a State Department employee. Chambers also claimed that Hiss had given him stolen documents that he passed on to the Soviets. Hiss, who denied the charges, could not be tried for espionage because of the statute of limitations. He was, however, convicted of perjury on January 21, 1950.

Outside the Washington, D.C., Beltway, "Red Scare" fears were centered on Hollywood. In 1947, HUAC began an investigation of the motion picture industry. Witnesses at the hearings named nineteen people in the industry who they claimed held left-wing views. Ten of those people, who became known as the Hollywood Ten, refused to testify before Congress, citing their Fifth Amendment rights. However, HUAC and the courts disagreed with the Hollywood Ten's refusal; the entire group, which included luminaries like screenwriters Dalton Trumbo and Ring Lardner Jr., was convicted of contempt of Congress and given prison sentences of six to twelve months. The Hollywood Ten and others in the industry who refused to name members of left-wing groups, such as Charlie Chaplin and Orson Welles, found themselves blacklisted and unable to find work.

McCarthy Steps onto the National Stage

Against that backdrop of spy and counterspy, Joseph McCarthy became a prominent public figure. McCarthy coveted the political limelight and was willing to shamelessly exploit groups and individuals to satisfy his thirst for power. He gained that power, at least for a time, by making accusations regarding the political affiliations, race, or sexual preferences of others. Because of the times, the easiest and fastest means to generate the nation's fear—and gain power for himself—was to accuse someone of being a Communist.

In 1948, McCarthy had said that his top priority was stopping the "spread of communism." Less than a month after Hiss's January 1950 conviction, McCarthy delivered the speech that would thrust him onto the national stage, declaring of the purported Communist infiltration of the State Department, "[We] are not dealing with spies who get 30 pieces of silver to steal the blueprints of a new weapon. We are dealing with a far more sinister type of activity because it permits the enemy to guide and shape our policy."

McCarthy's Wheeling speech prompted the establishment of a special Senate foreign relations committee, known informally as the Tydings Committee, to investigate his claims. Led by Millard Tydings, a Democratic senator from Maryland, the committee investigated the people McCarthy had brought to their attention. Of the nine people McCarthy had named publicly, the committee found that the senator offered no viable proof of their connection to the Communist Party. In addition, the committee reviewed the loyalty files of the State Department employees on McCarthy's list. In its report, issued on July 20, 1950, the committee concluded, "We have carefully and conscientiously reviewed each and every one of the loyalty files relative to the individuals charged by Senator McCarthy. In no instance was any one of them now employed in the State Department found to be 'a card-carrying Communist,' a member of the Communist Party, or 'loyal to the Communist Party.'"

Despite its findings, the Tydings Committee did little to squelch the rise of McCarthyism. In fact, Tydings became one of its first victims. The senator lost the 1950 election when a faked photo depicting him conversing with former Communist Party leader Earl Browder was distributed. The State Department also continued to be affected by accusations of communism. McCarthy's charges, issued with the authority he had as chairman of the Senate's Permanent Investigations Subcommittee, led to tighter security procedures, prompting the dismissal of several thousand employees in the early 1950s. Among them were John Carter Vincent and John Stewart Service. McCarthy continued to hold hearings, including one in 1953 to determine whether Communists were infiltrating Voice of America, a division of the U.S. Information Agency that broadcasts news and entertainment programs worldwide.

The Decline and Fall of McCarthy

McCarthy's popularity with the American public began to decline in March 1954 when journalist Edward R. Murrow presented a documentary of the senator on his television program *See It Now*. The show, filled mostly with clips of the senator, provided convincing evidence of McCarthy's abusive and berating tactics. A month after the broadcast, the Army-McCarthy hearings began, marking the final stages of McCarthy's demagoguery.

In October 1953, the Permanent Investigations Subcommittee had begun an investigation of alleged spying at the Fort Monmouth, New Jersey, army base. McCarthy, committee chair, claimed that Irving Peress, an army dentist, was given a promotion and honorable discharge after the army had learned of Peress's left-wing political views. When Secretary of the Army Robert T. Stevens was unable to convince McCarthy to call off the investigation, he charged that McCarthy and the subcommittee's chief counsel, Roy Cohn, had tried to procure special treatment, including an officer's commission, for Private G. David Schine, a recently drafted friend of Cohn. Stevens asserted that McCarthy and his staff were trying to harass the army into giving Schine a cushy domestic assignment. McCarthy and Cohn issued a countercharge, alleging that the army was delaying a decision on Schine in order to force the subcommittee to abandon its investigation. To allow the committee to investigate the charges, McCarthy gave up his chairmanship. However, he was allowed to cross-examine witnesses. The hearings began on April 22, 1954, and ended on June 17.

The hearings were seen by 20 million people, with live broadcasts on most ABC and DuMont (the original fourth network) affiliates; CBS and NBC offered nightly recaps. The thirty-two witnesses included General Miles Reber, the commanding general of the U.S. Army in Europe, who testified that McCarthy and Cohn had tried to pressure him into obtaining a commission for Schine, and Reber's brother Samuel, the high commissioner for the State Department in Germany. Other key witnesses included Major General Ralph Zwicker, the commanding officer at Fort Monmouth, and Soviet defector Alexander Barmine. Barmine and FBI informant Harvey Matusow were among the witnesses who supported McCarthy's allegations. However, Matusow would later recant his testimony.

McCarthy's stock did not rise because of his appearances on television. Both the audience in the Senate and those at home saw a man with a constant five o'clock shadow who repeatedly badgered witnesses and complained about being interrupted. McCarthy's abrasive behavior ultimately backfired when he began to question Frederick Fisher, a lawyer at army counsel Joseph Welch's law firm. The senator repeatedly harassed Fisher about his association with the National Lawyers Guild, a liberal association that had defended many targets of the Red Scare, including members of the Hollywood Ten. On June 9, an exasperated and tearful Welch finally exclaimed, famously, "Have you no sense of decency sir, at long last? Have you left no sense of decency?" Welch's outburst prompted applause by the spectators and sealed many people's opinion about the once-popular senator.

The End of the McCarthy Era

Following the hearings, the subcommittee issued four separate reports. Although both McCarthy and the army were cleared of most of the charges against them, the committee decided that Cohn had intervened too much in his effort to obtain preferential treatment for Schine. On July 20, Cohn resigned his position as chief counsel.

Even though he escaped punishment by the subcommittee, McCarthy still had problems. In July 1954, Republican senator Ralph E. Flanders, troubled by McCarthy's irresponsible claims of Communist infiltration in the military and government, introduced a resolution to censure his Wisconsin counterpart. On December 2, 1954, the Senate voted 67-22 to censure McCarthy on two charges: failing to cooperate in 1952 with a Senate subcommittee investigating McCarthy's private and political life, and bringing dishonor and disrepute to the Senate with his verbal attacks on his peers. McCarthy continued as a senator, but he became increasingly irrelevant. On May 2, 1957, he died of a liver ailment.

The Cold War has been over for more than a decade, and McCarthyism is a distant memory. However, the McCarthy era, especially the Army-McCarthy hearings, provides valuable lessons in understanding how fear can grip a nation at the expense of common sense and civil liberties. In *At Issue in History: The McCarthy Hearings*, the contributors explore the McCarthy era and its aftermath.

Chapter 1

Analyzing McCarthy's Methods

1

McCarthy's Use of Smearing and Intimidation

James A. Wechsler

James A. Wechsler was an editor and writer for the *New York Post* when he was called to testify before the McCarthy Committee in 1953. Wechsler, a lifelong journalist, freely admitted that he had joined the Young Communist League while a student at Columbia University in the 1930s, ultimately resigning his membership in 1937. Wechsler first found himself being questioned about some of his early writings during his youthful tenure as a Communist. Some of those books had been used by the U.S. Information Agency; the implication was that subversive material by Wechsler was quietly making its way into libraries. Then the subject turned to McCarthy's real concern—Wechsler's editorial position at the *Post*, which was critical of McCarthy and his methods. Wechsler soon realized that he was on trial for his editorial opinions. He marked this attack as the start of a dangerous new McCarthyist trend that would challenge the civil liberties of a free society. This account of the interview reveals some of McCarthy's most brutal techniques, including smear tactics, coercion, and intimidation.

When I entered McCarthy stood up stiffly and motioned me to the witness chair. Disarmingly, he asked me how I pronounced my last name. I was tempted to respond that he had pronounced it correctly on televi-

Excerpted from *The Age of Suspicion*, by James A. Wechsler (New York: Random House, 1953). Copyright © 1953 by James A. Wechsler. Reprinted by permission of the publisher.

sion but I resolved to fight such temptation. I answered the question. . . .

"I may say," he continued, speaking quite swiftly and softly so that I almost had difficulty hearing him, "the reason for your being called today is that you are one of the many authors of books whose books have been used in the Information Program in various libraries, and we would like to check into a number of matters. Mr. [Roy] Cohn will do the questioning."

Cohn took over briefly for a review of the names and dates of my published works. He elicited the fact that two of the books—*Revolt on the Campus* and *War Our Heritage*—were written when I was a member of the YCL [Young Communist League]. Then he jumped quickly to nonliterary fields and, during most of the remainder of the two hearings, little attention was devoted to the ostensible subject of the hearings—the books I had written. First he established that I had used the name "Arthur Lawson" on my YCL membership card.

"Let me add," I said, "that it was a name I was given when I joined and that I never used it again."

Cohn dropped the subject. Now he wanted to know how long I had been a member of the YCL. I gave him the answer and added that the whole chronology had already been published in the *Congressional Record* in the statement that Senator [Herbert H.] Lehman had inserted at my request.

The committee's researchers were apparently unaware of the existence of the document and wanted to know the date.

McCarthy seemed only mildly interested in Cohn's questioning; he was getting ready to take over himself. After another moment, he jumped in.

McCarthy Takes Over the Questioning

"May I interrupt, Mr. Cohn?" McCarthy asked and, without waiting for an answer, he interrupted at length, while Cohn maintained a sulky silence, like a star pupil whom teacher has pushed aside.

"Mr. Wechsler, do you have any other people who are members of the Young Communist League, who were or are members of the Young Communist League, working for you on your newspaper?"

The fight was beginning rather sooner than I had expected, and on ground I had hardly expected him to invade so casually.

This was the first of many questions that I answered fully despite my belief that they were far beyond the scope of the committee's authorized inquiry. I had resolved much earlier that silence was suicidal in dealing with McCarthy. I know some thoughtful people differ with me, and that there are some who believe I should have refused to answer any questions dealing with the policies and personnel of the newspaper I edit. But I was persuaded then, and I have not changed my opinion, that McCarthy was hoping I would refuse to testify so that he could use my silence to charge that I had something to hide. I was not trying to "convince" McCarthy of anything; I was trying to write a record that could be read intelligibly by bemused Americans who might still believe that McCarthy was interested in truth. To put it simply, I did not believe that my answers would tend to incriminate or degrade me but I was quite certain that silence would.

With that single stroke of . . ."brute brilliance," McCarthy thus virtually ruled out the whole structure of evidence which I had wide-eyedly assumed would resolve the issue once and for all.

"I will say that I am going to answer that question because I believe it is a citizen's responsibility to testify before a Senate committee whether he likes the committee or not," I said.

"I know you do not like this committee," McCarthy interjected tonelessly, as if to assure me at once that he was impervious to personal offense and as if he had forgotten that he had repeatedly refused to testify before a Senate committee because he considered it hostile to him.

"I want to say that I think you are now exploring a subject which the American Society of Newspaper Editors might want to consider at some length," I continued.

"I answer the question solely because I recognize your capacity for misinterpretation of a failure to answer. I answer it with the protest signified. To my knowledge there are no communists on the staff of the New York *Post* at this time."

What about former communists, McCarthy wanted to know. I identified them. There were four, and in each case they were men whose past affiliations were as well known as their present anti-communism.

Thus, in less than five minutes, an investigation allegedly directed at my work as an author of books in use by United States Information Service libraries had become an examination of the staff of the *Post*. There had been no indication as to what books of mine were found overseas, or any discussion of their content.

Now McCarthy got to his real point:

"You see your books, some of them, were paid for by taxpayers' money. They are being used, allegedly, to fight communism. Your record, as far as I can see it, has not been to fight communism. You have fought every man who has ever tried to fight communism, as far as I know. Your paper, in my opinion, is next to and almost paralleling the [Communist newspaper] *Daily Worker.* We are curious to know, therefore, why your books were purchased. We want to know how many communists, if any, you still have working for you."

This was quite a speech; it was a summary of everything that he had to say in that hearing and the one that followed. Listening to it I had to resist the competing emotions of anger and hopelessness. But I had brought with me a document that I naively considered a devastating rebuttal. Since McCarthy had delivered what almost sounded like his summation before the hearing had barely begun, I decided to use it at once.

Wechsler's Compelling Evidence Backfires

So I asked permission to insert in the record of the hearing the statement issued on December 28, 1952, by the National Committee of the Communist Party reviewing the previous election and especially the failure of the Progressive Party ticket to roll up a meaningful vote: it had in fact obtained only a small fraction of the disappointing Wallace vote of 1948. . . .

[The] communist jargon [of the statement] was simply a way of affirming what I had long believed—that the most effective opponents of communism in America have been the liberals and labor leaders associated with the noncommunist Left. Offering the document as an exhibit, I said: "I am rather fond of this tribute, and it may perhaps have some bearing on your comment that I have not been active in fighting communism."

In a cold, casual voice McCarthy responded quickly:

"Did you have anything to do with the passage of that resolution? Did you take any part in promoting the passage of that resolution?"

I thought I had expected anything, but my imagination had been inadequate. His words registered slowly. I must have looked baffled as well as astonished, almost incapable of trusting my own senses.

"Is that a serious question?" I asked.

McCarthy turned briskly to the stenographer.

"Will you read the question to the witness?"

His voice was harder and tougher. In this strange proceeding he alternately played the role of prosecutor and judge, and now he was definitely the prosecutor. The stenographer read the question.

He would not let go. "Do you feel that you may have been intimidated? Is there a doubt in your mind as to whether you have been intimidated?"

I knew I was making an obvious effort to keep my voice down as I answered, and I am sure my hands trembled a little:

"Sir, I have not been in any way affiliated with the communist movement since late 1937, as I believe your investigation will show. That resolution was adopted by the Communist Party as a tribute to the militant and vigorous anti-communism of the New York *Post* which has, in my judgment, been more effective in leading people away from communism, Senator, than those who prefer to identify liberalism with communism."

He let me finish and then, in the same flat tone, he said:

"Now will you answer the question?"

"The answer is no, Senator," I replied.

"The answer is no. Do you know whether anyone on your staff took part in promoting the passage of that resolution?"

"Senator, to the best of my knowledge, no one on my staff is a member of the Central Committee of the Communist Party or identified with it in any way."

"Now will you answer the question? Will you read the question to the witness?"

"I have answered it as best I can."

"You have said that you did not think anyone on your staff was a part of the committee. That was not the question. Read the question to the witness."

The stenographer read it. The faint smile which McCarthy had exhibited earlier was gone now. Once again, in a voice that must have sounded quite spiritless, I answered the question.

"I do not know that anyone on my staff took any part in promoting the passage of that resolution," I said. He had astounded me, and he knew it.

Thus, within ten minutes after the hearing had begun, I found myself in the preposterous position of denying under oath that I had inspired the long series of communist attacks against me, climaxed by the denunciation of the Central Committee.

With that single stroke of what Philip Graham, publisher of the Washington *Post*, later described as "brute brilliance," McCarthy thus virtually ruled out the whole structure of evidence which I had wide-eyedly assumed would resolve the issue once and for all. Here indeed was a daring new concept in which the existence of evidence of innocence becomes the damning proof of guilt. This is the way it must feel to be committed to a madhouse through some medical mistake; everything is turned upside down. What had heretofore constituted elementary reasonableness is viewed by everyone else as a quaint eccentricity; the most absurd remark becomes the commonplace.

McCarthy reverted to the same thesis several times. Each time he did so with total blandness, as though only the dullest or most subversive mind could detect anything extraordinary in his approach.

He had at last spelled out the formula under which our whole society could be transformed into a universe of suspicion. What a man had said or done could no longer be accepted as bearing the slightest relationship to what he was or what he believed. More likely, it was a disguise to conceal his hidden allegiances to exactly the reverse of what he claimed to stand for. At the second hearing he was to develop this theme even more spectacularly. . . .

Naming Names

Had I ever talked to the FBI? The answer was yes; whenever an FBI agent came to see me about someone I had known applying for a Government post, I gave as much information as I had; I always emphasized that I had no first-hand knowledge extending beyond 1937 and cautioned that others might have changed their views as decisively as I had. . . .

McCarthy seemed impatient as I responded:

"Where I have been asked about people I knew at that time [of my communist membership], I answered freely and fully. If I knew today that someone who had been in the Young Communist League with me was in a strategic Government post, I would certainly communicate that information. There has never been any question in my mind as to a citizen's responsibility on that point, and I do not believe the FBI would suggest that I have been uncooperative in the discussion of such cases."

But had I ever given the FBI a full list of everyone I had known?

The answer was that no such dragnet question, I am glad to say, had ever been asked me by the FBI. . . .

"Do you know any of those Young Communists who are in any Government position today?" McCarthy asked.

"No, I do not."

"Do you know Bernard De Voto?"

"I trust this is not a sequitur," I replied.

"Pardon?"

"I trust this is not a sequitur."

"It is a question."

"I believe I may have met Bernard De Voto. I can't recall the occasion on which I did. I regret to say that he is not a close personal friend of mine."

"You regret to say that?"

"Yes, sir."

"You did not collaborate with him in writing the article in which he advocated that Americans not talk to the FBI?"

"No, sir, I thought that was a very bad article."

"You do not agree with that?"

"I don't agree with that."

This exchange compressed into half a minute a whole range of McCarthy devices. First there was the sudden introduction of De Voto's name into a discussion dealing with the identity of former communists; he happens to be a distinguished American scholar who never roamed into communist territory. Then there was the intimation that De Voto's article on the FBI was proof he was a traitor and that I not only sanctioned the article but had helped him write it (presumably in that spare time when I was not writing communist denunciations of myself). It was almost a case of guilt by non-association.

The Final Gambit

Then McCarthy announced:

"We are going to ask you, Mr. Wechsler, to prepare a list and submit it to the committee and consider it to be submitted under oath, of all the Young Communist Leaguers that you knew as such, or the communists."

This was the final gambit. I had characterized myself as a "responsible but not friendly witness." From the start, whether rightly or wrongly, I had believed that what McCarthy was seeking was the chance to walk out of the hearing room and tell the press that I had "balked." Once he was able to do that, I would be engaged in the hopeless pursuit of headlines describing me as just another reluctant witness. And from that point on McCarthy would proceed to discredit the *Post* because I had refused to testify freely before a Senate committee.

There may be some splendor in such a role but on the whole it escapes me. By and large liberals have believed in giving wide scope to congressional committees. Moreover, there is in the American tradition a very real belief that the man who has nothing to conceal will speak up when spoken to; muteness has not often been equated with valor. Back in 1947, in an article in the *Guild Reporter,* I had written:

> It would be nice if the world were prettier, but it isn't; espionage and sabotage are facts of modern life. I have no brief for anybody who refuses to testify before a congressional committee; no matter how foolish or fierce the committee, an American ought to be prepared to state his case in any public place at any time.

Believing this, I had gone along answering everything and now I faced what McCarthy undoubtedly regarded as the great question. I am sure that he knew enough about me to guess the reluctance with which I would give such a list to a man like him. I am also confident that he would have felt he had finally cornered me if I now refused to give it to him. Then, and for many days after, it was a rather strange duel. For McCarthy knew I would have been happier not to give him any list and I knew he would have been delighted if I had taken that stand.

All this, let me add, was clearer to me after the hearing than at that moment. The demand for the list was an almost parenthetical remark; my answer was an oblique comment about the obvious absurdity of asking a man to remember everyone whom he had known in a different context nearly sixteen years before.

"I don't know that you would be able to do very well with a similar list of any organization that you were connected with sixteen years ago," I said.

"Well, we are asking for the list. You say you have severed your connection. I am not going to, at this time, try to—"

"Senator, you are raising that point," I interrupted.

He went on as if I were inaudible.

"—pass on whether that is true or not. I know that you never testified in a case against an ex-communist. I know that none of the men you have named here as anti-communists ever testified in a case against communists. I know that they and you have been consistently and viciously attacking anyone who does testify against communists, anyone that exposes communists—"

"Senator, that is not true."

"Let me finish. You may have all the time in the world to talk. So you cannot blame the average person who questions whether you ever did break with the party."

There it was again, and not for the last time; and each time he said it I had a feeling of rage tinged with futility. . . .

McCarthy as a Calculating Demagogue

Throughout the interrogation the grand inquisitor was by turns truculent, contemptuous and bland. Yet I rarely had any feeling of authentic personal animosity. He acted like the gangster in a B-movie who faces the unpleasant necessity of rubbing out someone who has gotten in his way: he would really like the victim to feel that there is nothing personal about it and that he rather regrets the exorbitant demands of duty. At no time did I have the feeling that I was confronted by a fanatic. McCarthy is a poker player, not a zealot, a cold-blooded operator in a big game. There were a few off-the-record asides when he almost seemed to be saying: "Look, don't get excited, old man, we've all got our rackets." This detachment may be his greatest strength; at moments it endows him with a certain cold charm. . . .

It looked as though we were nearing the end.

"Have You Been Intimidated?"

"As I recall, and I may misquote this, because I do not read your sheet," McCarthy said, "I understand that you have been disturbed by the unfair treatment witnesses received before this committee. Do you feel you were unfairly treated?"

He asked the question almost clinically, like a doctor asking a patient whether the needle he had just administered was really painful.

"Senator, I question the basic nature of this proceeding, of course I do," I replied.

"You feel you were unfairly treated?"

"I regard this proceeding as the first in a long line of attempts to intimidate editors who do not equate McCarthyism with patriotism."

Again he betrayed no resentment over the used of the word "McCarthyism"; I think he is rather proud to be an ism as well as a Senator.

"You have not been intimidated, have you?" he persisted.

"Senator, I am a pretty tough guy," I responded with a certain vanity.

"I say you have not been intimidated, have you?"

"I say this is the first of a long line of attempts to do so," I answered.

"Answer my question. Have you been intimidated?"

"You are not going to win this argument, Senator. We will go back and forth all afternoon."

It was getting to be a comic colloquy, but he wasn't smiling. He seemed genuinely absorbed in the line of questioning. I think one of his true delights is the constant rediscovery of his own strength. For public purposes he may have wanted to wrest a statement that I had not been terrorized, yet I think he would have been equally happy to hear me say that I had been.

"Have you been intimidated?" he repeated in the same phlegmatically insistent voice.

"Sir, I have been taken away from my work. I have not even had a chance to write a word about Senator McCarthy today."

He smiled then; the picture of anyone writing about him could not be unattractive. He hammered back:

"You have not been intimidated at all, have you? You mean you have been inconvenienced. The question is: 'Have you been intimidated?'"

He was provoking me into a speech.

"I am fully aware this is a proceeding designed to smear the New York *Post*," I said. "I recognize that, Senator. We are both grown up. But this is a free country and I am going to keep fighting."

"So will the *Daily Worker* and every other communist-line paper," he responded. "But have you been intimidated?"

"I am afraid that is a question we would have to discuss with doctors and get all sorts of expert testimony."

"In other words, you cannot answer that question?"

It was like being a small child and having the town bully ask you whether you have had enough. No answer you can give him is satisfactory to yourself; for if you say that you haven't been frightened, you may re-enforce his sense of virtue, and if you say that you have been he can walk away triumphant. So I clung to the evasive answer.

"I say there is no doubt that this is an attempt to intimidate me. I trust that I have the moral courage to stand up under it. I trust that other editors will."

He would not let go.

"Do you feel that you may have been intimidated? Is there a doubt in your mind as to whether you have been intimidated?"

"We will not know, Senator, until we see whether as editor of the *Post* I keep on fighting just as hard for the things I believe as I have been. I think I will."

"Do you think you have been intimidated?" he asked monotonously.

"I have great confidence in myself, so at the moment, Senator, I feel I have not been intimidated."

"Do you feel you have been abused?"

"Why of course I have been abused. The suggestion that my break with communism was not authentic is the greatest affront you could recite anywhere. I have fought this battle a long time, longer than you have, Senator, and I have taken plenty of beatings from the communists in the course of that fight. So I feel very strongly about this."

McCarthy's Double Role

Now he spoke in the accents of a judge who, having listened to the devastating words of the prosecutor, delivers his verdict:

"I may say, so that there is no doubt in your mind, so that you need not say that Senator McCarthy intimated or insinuated that you have not broken: I have been following your record, not as closely perhaps as I would if you were in Government, but I have been following you somewhat. I am convinced that you have done exactly what you would do if you were a member of the Communist Party, if you wanted to have a phony break and then use that phony break to the advantage of the Communist Party. I feel that you have not broken with Communist ideals. I feel that you are serving them very, very actively. Whether you are doing it knowingly or not, that is in your own mind. I have no knowledge as to whether you have a card in the party."

I had vowed not to explode; I said as derisively as I could:

"I appreciate that concession."

He ignored the sarcasm; he was very much the judge now, handing down the decision in favor of the prosecutor (who happened to be himself) and untroubled by any murmuring in the courtroom.

"I think you are doing tremendous damage to America," he continued, "when I find books by authors like yourself being purchased by the Information Program we are going to check into them. I say this so you need not say that McCarthy intimated or insinuated. McCarthy did not intimate, he said that he thinks Wechsler is still very, very valuable to the Communist Party.". . .

There was a perfunctory aftermath. Senator [Henry] Jackson asked me a few additional questions that enabled me to introduce the remaining exhibits I had brought with me. Roy Cohn got around to asking me about Reed Harris, and I gave the unsatisfactory answer he had anticipated; anything I had to say about Harris was favorable, and Cohn didn't labor the inquiry.

With McCarthy gone the spirit had left the hearing. To debate with Roy Cohn appeared to be the climactic foolishness of the fantastic afternoon. Senator Jackson did not need additional documentation. His problem was how to deal with Joe McCarthy.

It was all over at 5:40, ninety minutes after we had begun.

2

McCarthy Unfairly Attacked Innocent Witnesses

Charles E. Potter

Senator Charles E. Potter served one term in the Senate. As a Republican, he sat as a majority member on McCarthy's Permanent Subcommittee on Investigations during the infamous Army-McCarthy hearings. Although he shared party affiliation with McCarthy, Potter was known for holding an ambivalent view of the Wisconsin senator's controversial actions. In this critical retrospective account of the proceedings, Potter describes in detail McCarthy's attack on the first army witness, Major General Miles Reber, including the senator's ruthless smearing of the general's brother. The account provides a firsthand demonstration of McCarthy's expert smearing technique.

The McCarthy episode was, short of war, one of the most dramatic and provocative events in this century if not in all American history. It is unlikely that fate will ever again assemble a similar cast or write a comparable script.

The story reached its climax in the spring of 1954 when a cloud of terror blanketed the United States. Like a gigantic, tumultuous hurricane it dominated the thoughts and actions of the American people, disrupting their emotions, distorting their judgment. Sanity seemed to go into hiding, opinions whirled to the outer edges of human thought. There was no compromise, no courage to laugh at the basic absurdity. Even now [the mid-1960s], pockets of

Excerpted from *Days of Shame*, by Charles E. Potter (New York: Coward-McCann, Inc., 1965). Copyright © 1965 by Charles E. Potter. Reprinted with permission.

this strange phenomenon are evident.

At the center of the disturbance, stimulating the confusion and pumping power into the dissension was one man—Joseph Raymond McCarthy, junior Senator from Wisconsin—a brutal demagogue to some, a godlike savior to others. To no one was he unimportant.

As a United States Senator from Michigan and a member of the Senate Government Operations Committee, it was my privilege to live through those days in the center of the action. I was, along with McCarthy and Senators [Everett] Dirksen and [Karl] Mundt, one of the majority GOP members of the committee. The Democrats were Senators [John L.] McClellan, [Stuart] Symington, and [Henry] Jackson.

The pattern for the final act in McCarthy's uproarious career began with the attempts of a legal counsel of the committee (Roy Cohn) to save his friend (G. David Schine) from serving his country as an Army private.

From this simple and selfish whim of two young men who seemed to be demonstrating a rare kind of irresponsibility, the entire country was swept into a tornado of emotional nonsense. It turned husband against wife, brother against brother, changed close friends into snarling enemies, disrupted the political pattern of the Nation and sent messages over all the oceans that the United States had gone stark, raving mad.

The hearings spurted a strange, psychotic force into millions of American homes.

Each citizen found he must declare himself, stand up and be counted. He must be either "for" McCarthy or "against" him. Somehow it had been arranged—almost, it seemed, by cosmic direction—that if you were for him you were a "red-blooded patriot"; if not, you were a "Commie lover."

In the late spring of 1954, a committee hearing, featuring Senator McCarthy vs the United States Army, became the focal point of the Nation. The controversy had raced far beyond the question of whether or not David Schine should be required to serve his country like any other young man. This was McCarthyism on trial.

The hearings spurted a strange, psychotic force into

millions of American homes. The reputations of dozens of people, both prominent and unimportant, were scarred. The rule book went out the window and no referee could control Joe McCarthy. . . .

Point of Order

"A point of order, Mr. Chairman."

That was the first time we heard it, the first time many millions of Americans, their eyes glued to the other end of the television apparatus, would hear and see Joe McCarthy bring up his endless points of order. His puffed eyelids, his tight upper lip that never moved when he talked, the stone cold eyes and the front hair grown long and slicked back over his balding head would dominate these hearings for the next ten weeks.

He knew where the cameras were located and he was always certain to be facing one as he made his endless points of order. Most of them were improper.

McCarthy's point of order was his objection that the specifications in the Army charges were entitled, "Filed by the Department of the Army." It wasn't the Army, he said, but [Robert] Stevens, [John] Adams, and [H. Struve] Hensel who were bringing the charges, not the Army. These three were not the Army but were "Pentagon politicians" attempting to disrupt his investigations. He said that it was a disgrace and a reflection upon a million outstanding men in the Army to let a few civilians, who were "trying to hold up an investigation of Communists," label themselves the Department of the Army. [The charges were that McCarthy, Cohn, and other members of the Permanent Subcommittee on Investigations had tried, via improper means, to get preferential treatment for Private Schine.]

I began to feel sorry for Karl Mundt. He just was not capable of controlling McCarthy. But—who was?

Joe was on camera now; he had the audience and he was certain that out there many millions of people were believing him, were nodding their heads over the ludicrous charge that Stevens and the others were, indeed, coddling Communists. . . .

The First Witness: Major General Miles Reber

The first witness was Major General Miles Reber, at that time the Commanding General of the United States Army in Europe. He had been flown to Washington from his headquarters in Kaiserslautern, Germany, to appear at the hearing. Flying General Reber back and forth to Europe so that he might testify for a few minutes at this hearing was just a small fraction of the idiotic expenses with which the public of the United States was charged.

But once again before the hearings could move on in an orderly way, Joe McCarthy decided to cause another commotion. Struve Hensel, Assistant Secretary of Defense, was sitting next to Miles Reber. Two days before, McCarthy had suddenly taken a wild swing at Hensel, accusing him of launching the Army report to block, Joe said, exposure of Hensel's "misconduct and possible law violation which was being investigated by his subcommittee." Once again, this was news to all us other six members of the subcommittee. Hensel, McCarthy charged, had helped organize a ships' supply firm which sold goods in an illegal way to the U.S. Navy during World War II when Hensel was a Navy official.

Hensel answered that the charge was a "barefaced lie." McCarthy, Hensel said, "is cornered and is pursuing his usual tactics. If he cares to repeat the charges against me without his Senate immunity, I will sue him."

Finally, having made his point over radio and television, McCarthy dismissed the entire question as unimportant and pompously said he would withdraw it.

McCarthy was in Houston that day for a speech and was asked by United Press if he would repeat the charge openly. He refused.

A long time later Joe admitted that his charges against Hensel were as phony as a three-dollar bill and that he had learned this type of strategy from an old friend whom he called Indian Charlie. Whenever Charlie was in a tight spot, Joe said, he would first kick his adversary in the genitals and then go on to more normal discussions.

Now, at the hearing, Joe demanded that Reber identify his "counsel" sitting next to him. This, as Joe knew it would, infuriated Hensel who said that he was not Reber's counsel and that McCarthy knew well who he was.

Joe's nervous giggle spread through the microphone to the far walls of the Caucus Room. His eyes flicked to the TV cameras like a burlesque comedian who has scored with a laugh.

Reber told the hearings that he had been called to Joe's office in July where both Joe and Roy Cohn had urged that a commission be obtained for David Schine. And that during that first conversation Cohn had told him that Schine had been a junior ship's officer in the Army Transport Service and had served in that capacity for approximately a year in 1946, on the U.S. Army transport *General Widner*.

This was not true. Schine had been a purser and a civilian.

Reber said that he had been urged by both McCarthy and Cohn to go into full-speed-ahead action because Schine was now on the ready list to be drafted.

The Pentagon guessed rightly, and Reber did testify, that never before had he been under such pressure to obtain a commission for a rookie soldier although his office processed an average of a thousand a week. . . .

Joseph Welch, special counsel for the Army, wasted no time with Reber in his first active part in the hearing.

WELCH: General Reber, I think I have about three questions for you. Were you acutely aware of Mr. Cohn's position as counsel for this committee in the course of your conversation and contacts with him?

REBER: I was, Mr. Welch.

WELCH: Did that position occupied by Mr. Cohn increase or diminish the interest with which you pursued the problem?

REBER: To the best of my ability, I feel that it increased the interest.

WELCH: One more question, sir. Disregarding the word "improper" influence or pressure, do you recall any instance comparable to this in which you were put under greater pressure?

REBER: To the best of my recollection, I recall of no instance under which I was put under greater pressure.

McCarthy Slanders Reber's Brother

Then the fireworks began.

There was nothing startling or defamatory about Reber's testimony. He had performed with the efficiency and

dignity that we had learned to expect from West Point officers appearing before committees. But there must have
been something about an Army officer, and particularly this
type of Army officer, that infuriated McCarthy. After the
questioning had gone around the committee twice and
there seemed to be nothing more needed from this witness,
Joe gave the hearings another injection of Indian Charlie.

"Is Sam Reber your brother?"

General Reber was startled as was everyone else in the
room. Did anything about Sam Reber's activities make the
general acutely aware of the fact that Mr. Cohn was chief
counsel of the committee? Joe wanted to know. General Reber, wary now, said no.

McCarthy then asked: "Do you know that Mr. Sam Reber was the superior to Mr. Kaghan, that Mr. Cohn and Mr.
Schine were sent by me to Europe to inspect the libraries,
that your brother, Mr. Sam Reber, repeatedly made attacks
upon them, and that your brother, Mr. Sam Reber, appointed a man to shadow them throughout Europe and
keep the press informed as to where they were going and
where they were stopping? Were you aware of that at the
time you were making this great effort to get consideration,
as you say, for Mr. Schine?"

(Samuel Reber had been Acting High Commissioner
for the State Department in Germany at the time of the
Cohn-Schine trip. The "shadow" appointed by Reber had
been an official of the Visitors Bureau who arranged, at the
request of Cohn and Schine, the details of their plane
schedules, appointments and hotel rooms. The "attacks"
had been Sam Reber's refusal to denounce Ted Kaghan as a
"Communist sympathizer." Kaghan had been respected as
one of the most effective organizers of anti-Communist
propaganda in Germany.)

The storm simmered down for a minute and McCarthy
asked Reber if, at the time he was processing the application
of David Schine, he was aware of the fact that Schine had
had a very unpleasant experience with Reber's brother, who
was then Acting High Commissioner for the United States
in Germany. Reber answered that he had known of no such
episode although he was aware that Cohn and Schine had
had specific difficulties with the Department of State.

McCarthy backed away from Sam Reber for a few minutes and made the mistake of referring to the original meet-

ing between himself, Reber and Cohn, and emphasizing the point that Reber had said he had thought Schine would be entitled to a commission. This gave Reber the opportunity to testify that he had thought so too because Roy Cohn had told him that Schine had served as a junior ship's officer. If that had been true, Reber now testified, Schine might have been commissioned.

Joe was groping now. "General, you were before this committee a number of times, is that right, when I was chairman?"

"I actually only testified, Senator McCarthy, once—on the 8th of September, 1953," Reber replied.

Then Joe seemed to fly off into outer space.

MCCARTHY: At that time I asked you—as I recall—I repeated the question a number of times—asked you whether or not you felt that the committee should be entitled to the names of individuals in the Pentagon who had protected and covered up Communists. At that time I had difficulty getting an answer from you on that. I ask you this question today because I am firmly convinced the reason we are spending our time on the question of whether or not Private Schine received special consideration is because we are getting close to the nerve center in the Pentagon of the old civilian politicians over the past ten or twenty years who have covered up. I want to ask you today whether or not you feel that this committee, when we get through with this television show, should be entitled to get the names of those, for example, who received the cases of individuals who had been suspended from Fort Monmouth. I am not speaking of the 33 suspensions during our investigations. I am speaking of investigations made long before that, over the past five, six, or seven years by competent commanding officers—I believe the figure was 35, I am not sure—by different commanding officers, who were found unfit by the First Army Loyalty Board because of Communist background. They applied to a screening board or an appeal board or a loyalty board, I don't know what you would call it, in the Pentagon; and of the 35, 33 . . .

Mundt rescued him. "The Senator's time has expired."

I had watched Reber and Cohn through this droning, pointless monologue, delivered in that strange, tight-upper-lipped, overdramatic voice that Joe never used unless there was an audience or a camera in range. They were both trying to follow what he was saying, but first puzzlement, then apprehension, then a shadow of pity seemed to hit them both. There was something of disgust, too, evident in Cohn, a literate man being forced to listen to a pretty terrible script.

Mundt then asked for further questions from the six of us. Only Symington accepted the offer to bring out testimony that General Reber, under his oath of office, would have acted entirely in accordance with that oath no matter what might have happened to his brother or anyone else. We adjourned then until after lunch, and I was happy for a few moments that McCarthy's ugly punch at Sam Reber was apparently ended. I soon learned that this was only the beginning.

McCarthy's Expert Smearing Technique

Roy Cohn took over the questioning as the afternoon session opened. He made a minor attempt to score a point by bringing out that no Army report similar to the one charging him and McCarthy had been filed by the Army after Captain Irving Peress had asked to have his overseas orders canceled because his wife and daughter were ill. Cohn was off side on the play, and he knew it and did not press it.

Henry Jackson brought out from Reber that at no time during the long negotiations over the commissioning of David Schine had Roy Cohn, or anyone else, complained to him about any alleged bias connected with his brother. The general said that the first time he had ever heard either McCarthy or Cohn mention his brother was at this hearing.

Then it was McCarthy's turn again and he had apparently been refueling at the Carroll Arms Hotel during the lunch period. Out the window went all the rules of this particular hearing, of any hearing.

"Are you aware," Joe demanded, "of the fact that your brother was allowed to resign when charges that he was a bad security risk were made against him as a result of the investigations of this committee?"

This was news to the other six members of the committee, and, I am sure, news to Joe until this moment.

[Subcommittee counsel] Ray Jenkins jumped in with an objection on the grounds that the question was wholly irrelevant, which it certainly was.

McCarthy, totally washed free of any courtesy now, interrupted to say that if Reber's brother was forced to resign as a bad security risk, it should be on the record as a possible motive for his testimony.

McClellan objected, pointing out that there was no testimony that the statements McCarthy was making were true and until they were proved true, McCarthy's question to Reber was incompetent. Ray Jenkins said McCarthy was entitled to ask Reber whether or not the statements were true.

Finally, having made his point over radio and television, McCarthy dismissed the entire question as unimportant and pompously said he would withdraw it.

This time it was the witness, General Reber, who objected and asked for permission to answer the serious charge against his brother. The squabbling continued for two hours with Ray Jenkins contributing the strange observation that he thought General Reber was in error in saying that a serious attack had been made on his brother because no proof had been introduced by McCarthy. Jenkins did not mention that upwards of twenty million Americans had heard the serious slander of Samuel Reber. That was the McCarthy technique.

Henry Jackson recognized this and said that McCarthy's distorted charges against Samuel Reber could be stricken from the record but could not be stricken from the newspapers, the television audience and the radio audience. He thought Miles Reber should be given the opportunity to answer.

McCarthy snarled at Jackson, made a wild statement that he and Roy Cohn had been accused of everything except "murdering our great-great-grandmother" and said that he had a duty, not a right but a duty, to show the motive of the witness.

Stuart Symington interrupted to say that he did not understand what General Reber's brother had to do with General Reber with respect to telephone calls that may have been made, properly or improperly, because his brother may or may not have been a security risk. This was a cold dash of logic and sanity squirted into the hurricane that McCarthy was attempting to create, and we heard no more about it.

Finally General Reber was allowed to speak. "I merely wanted to say that, as I understand my brother's case, he retired as he is entitled to do by law upon reaching the age of fifty. That is all I wanted to say. I know nothing about any security case involving him."

There was, of course, no security investigation against Samuel Reber. This senseless slander of his name had resulted from the seventeen-day tour of Europe by Roy Cohn and David Schine, an episode that had made the United States the laughingstock of the world. Several thousand dollars which belonged to the public had been poured down the drain, and the pouring had been approved by Joe McCarthy without mentioning a word of it to any other member of the committee that was supposed to be sponsoring the tour.

As soon as Reber was able to get his statement on the record, Karl Mundt hastily dismissed him from the witness stand, and McCarthy turned to a snapping debate with Jackson over the date on which [FBI agent] Francis Carr had been appointed to the [McCarthy] staff. It was a minor squabble but it did put on the record another instance of perjury. There would be many many more in the ten weeks to come.

3

McCarthy Defends His Actions

Joseph R. McCarthy

Joseph R. McCarthy (1908–1957) served in the U.S. Senate from 1947 until his death. In 1950 McCarthy embarked on a crusade against communism. He eventually presided as chairman on the Permanent Subcommittee on Investigations, holding infamous public hearings in which he accused government employees and officials, army officers, and members of the media of Communist subversion. McCarthy was censured by the Senate in 1954, after which he continued as a senator, albeit without his influential base of power.

Before he became chairman of his own committee, McCarthy served as a minority member on the Tydings Committee, which in 1950 investigated McCarthy's initial charges of Communist infiltration within the State Department. The Tydings Committee eventually concluded that the Wisconsin senator's charges were unfounded and fraudulent. In this excerpt from his own book, McCarthy publishes his responses to questions he was frequently asked about the proceedings of the committee and attempts to explain his doctrine of guilt by association.

What was the Tydings Committee and why was it set up?

The Tydings Committee was set up as a result of information which I gave the Senate about the Communist connections of a sizable number of present and past State Department employees. I gave the Senate a brief review of the

Excerpted from *McCarthyism: The Fight for America, Documented Answers to Questions Asked by Friend and Foe*, by Joseph R. McCarthy (New York: The Devin-Adair Company, 1952). Copyright © 1952 by Joseph R. McCarthy. Reprinted by permission of the publisher.

files of 81 individuals who were then or had been closely connected with the State Department. At that time I informed the Senate that I did not have the staff, the power of subpoena, or the facilities to produce all of the available evidence against those individuals, but that the evidence which I had clearly indicated that many of them were either Communists or doing the work of the Communist Party. Others were marginal cases who might be able to prove their loyalty.

The Senate thereupon voted unanimously that the Foreign Relations Committee should hold hearings. It ordered that committee to subpoena all of the files on those named by me. The Tydings Committee was given all the money, investigators, and power it needed to do the job.

The Tydings Committee was, of course, carefully selected to do the job which it finally did. At that time there was in existence a Special Senate Investigating Committee fully staffed with competent investigators which could have done the job. The Judiciary Committee, headed by a great American who is anti-Communist, Senator Pat McCarran, also could have done the job. But the Foreign Relations Committee was selected. The reason for choosing that committee can best be described in the words of ex-Senator Scott Lucas when he said on the Senate floor:

> All we are trying to do is to give the Committee on Foreign Relations jurisdiction of the proposed investigation, rather than have the Committee on the Judiciary or the Committee on Expenditures in the Executive Departments, or some other committee immediately take jurisdiction . . .

Here we have notification from Democrat Leader Lucas that the reason for selecting the Tydings Committee was to make sure that no other committee would go into the matter. It seemed obvious in view of this that the committee was not formed to make a complete investigation but to prevent a real investigation. Why the Administration feared an investigation has, of course, since become obvious.

The Tydings Committee was ordered to obtain all of the files which might contain information on those you named. What files were they supposed to get?

State Department files, Civil Service Commission files, FBI files, Naval Intelligence files, Army Intelligence files, Secret Service files, and Central Intelligence Agency files.

Did the Tydings Committee obey the order of the Senate and subpoena all the files?

No.

What, if any, files were obtained by the Tydings Committee?

The loose leaf State Department files.

Why the Files Were Incomplete

Why were not the files of the Central Intelligence Agency, Civil Service Commission, FBI, Naval Intelligence, Army Intelligence, and Secret Service subpoenaed by the Committee?

In this respect Tydings should not take the full blame because the President publicly announced that he would defy the Senate subpoena for the loyalty files, saying he would stand pat on his 1948 order instructing all government departments to refuse to let Congress look at loyalty records of Government employees. At the same time President Truman indicated that he would make available any files which would *disprove* Senator McCarthy's charges of Communist infiltration.

In other words, if a file would prove that a man was guilty of treason or Communist activities, the Committee, according to Truman, could not see that file. If the file would prove that McCarthy was wrong then the file could be seen by the committee.

You have stated that the loose leaf State Department files which the Tydings Committee obtained had been stripped of all information about Communist activities before they were shown to the committee. Tydings claimed this was untrue. What evidence do you have to support your claim?

I gave to the Senate and to the Tydings Committee the written statements of four of the State Department employees—one of whom is now an FBI agent—who did the actual job of removing from the State Department files all evidence of Communist activities. . . .

Tydings denied that the files had been tampered with—in spite of those signed statements. He refused to call Paul Sullivan or any of the four who stated they were willing to testify under oath that they themselves had removed material in State Department files. He announced he was calling on the Department of Justice to tell him whether the files had been stripped or tampered with.

On June 21, Tydings told newspaper reporters that "a special inquiry by the FBI has established as false McCarthy's accusations that the files had been raped, skeletonized, or tampered with in any way.". . . .

The matter would have ended there had not I decided to ask J. Edgar Hoover, the head of the FBI, about this. Mr. Hoover replied on July 10 that this was not true—that the FBI had not made an investigation of the files during the time the files were available to the committee.

"The Federal Bureau of Investigation has made no such examination," Mr. Hoover wrote, "and therefore is not in a position to make any statement concerning the completeness or incompleteness of the State Department files.". . . .

The President publicly announced that he would defy the Senate subpoena for the loyalty files.

Hoover's statement, the direct opposite of Tydings', was taken to the floor of the Senate and presented so all the country could see.

Had it not been for J. Edgar Hoover's frank and honest report the truth never would have been known. . . .

If the Tydings Committee was formed for the purpose of investigating your charges of Communists in Government, why was not all of your evidence given to that Committee?

Being a member of the Minority Party, I had no control whatsoever over the Tydings Committee. I had no power to order the Tydings Committee to hear evidence which it did not want to hear. We had available some thirty witnesses who were willing to testify under oath as to the Communistic activities, associations, and connections of those whom I had named. Senator [Bourke] Hickenlooper asked Tydings to call those witnesses. This Tydings refused to do.

The evidence of Robert Morris, Minority Counsel, was repeatedly rejected by the chairman. For example, in one case, Morris said:

There is a case of a man named Theodore Geiger. He has been an employee of the State Department. He is now one of Paul Hoffman's top assistants. He is doing work that is quasi-State Department in character. I have gone and gotten some witnesses together who will testify that he was a member of the same Communist Party unit as they were, and I think we would be delinquent if in the face of this evidence that is now on record . . .

To this, Tydings replied: "Turn it over to the FBI or do something else with it . . . We don't want to waste this afternoon."

After Chairman Tydings refused to call the witnesses, the Democrat majority issued a report saying that I failed to prove my case. About the only analogy I can think of is that of a judge who refuses to hear any of the plaintiff's testimony and then renders a decision against him, saying he has failed to prove his case.

You were a judge. Why was not more "court room" proof presented on those you named?

A vast amount of legal proof was offered to the committee. Names of important witnesses were given to the committee with the request that they be called.

Failure to Call Witnesses

The following is an excellent illustration of the committee's failure to call witnesses.

Senator Hickenlooper challenged the committee on June 28, 1950, on its failure to call witnesses. He said he felt that the committee could not arrive at any final conclusion about my charges unless they called a list of witnesses which had been suggested to them. To this reasonable suggestion Senator [Theodore Francis] Green replied sarcastically that the committee did not place "want ads" in the paper to find witnesses, adding, "It seems to me that we have done all that we need to do in connection with the job that was imposed on us."

Senator Hickenlooper then reminded Green that the committee had not called the list of 20 or 30 names of witnesses he wanted to testify before the committee.

Incidentally, a number of the witnesses whom Tydings refused to call—such as General Alexander Barmine, who testified as to [Owen] Lattimore's connection with Russian military intelligence—have since been called and testified under oath before the McCarran Committee.

A huge amount of documentary evidence—such as photostats of checks, letters, memoranda, signed affidavits and statements—was offered to the Tydings Committee. Leads on other evidence were also given that committee. Those leads were never followed up even though the committee had a staff of investigators. Instead those investigators spent months investigating or trying to discredit McCarthy. . . .

Failure to Intelligently Cross-Examine Witnesses

Despite the fact that I had been spending practically 18 hours a day for months on this subject, I was denied the right to examine or cross-examine even a single witness.

The Tydings Committee, on the other hand, had the full power to examine and cross-examine both friendly and hostile witnesses but completely failed to develop the evidence which is normally developed by careful examination of the witnesses.

As a member of the Minority Party, which controls no committees, you knew that you could not force the appearance of any witnesses unless the Democrat chairman was willing to subpoena them. Therefore, why didn't you wait until the Republicans were in control of the Senate so that you could produce all of the evidence instead of doing it in a piecemeal pattern which a member of the political party not in power must of necessity follow?

I suggest you put yourself in my position. If you were a Senator of the Minority Party who knew of individuals high in government who were betraying this nation, could you sleep on the evidence and refuse to give it to the public because you were not allowed to produce a complete "court room" case? Would you not feel you owed the duty to the people whom you represented to make public the evidence which might save our nation from further disaster? If you were in my position you could either follow the example of Nero and fiddle while Western civilization burned, or you could attempt to form a bucket brigade and wade in and try to put out the fire even though firebugs or arsonists were in charge of the Fire Department—even though you knew you might get badly burned—even though the odds were against success.

The report of the Tydings Committee signed by the three Democrats states that your evidence of Communists in the State Department was a "fraud and a hoax." Is not the average American justified in assuming that this report signed by three Democrat Senators is true?

Obviously, . . . it is impossible to give all of the vast amount of evidence against those named. For that reason, I shall take a typical case and let you decide whether the evidence is a "fraud and a hoax."

One of the cases given the Tydings Committee by me was that of William Remington. Remington at that time was on the Commerce Department payroll, but working closely with the State Department. The following excerpt from the Senate resolution shows that the Tydings Committee was ordered by the Senate to examine cases such as Remington's:

> . . . the committee is directed to procure by subpoena and examine the complete loyalty and employment files and records of all the Government employees in the Department of State, *and such other agencies against whom charges have been heard.* (Emphasis mine.)

After the Tydings Committee had cleared Remington and declared my evidence was a "fraud and a hoax," a grand jury indicted him on the grounds that he lied when he denied membership in the Communist Party. A jury of 12 men and women, by a vote of 12 to 0, decided that he had perjured himself when he stated that he had not been a member of the Communist Party. This perhaps better than any documents of mine should help the average American decide whether McCarthy was right when he gave evidence of Communists in government, or whether the Tydings Committee was right when it said that my evidence that men such as Remington were Communists was a "fraud and a hoax."

The Tydings Committee, of course, was not alone in refusing to recognize that there were Communists in government. It should be remembered that when the evidence on Alger Hiss was being made public, the President gave Hiss a clean bill of health by stating on a number of occasions that the Hiss case was merely a "red herring."

The Tydings Report has been called a "Whitewash Report." Can you give me one specific example of any "whitewashing" that committee did?

Yes. Take the case of Haldore Hanson.

Haldore Hanson was a State Department employee who was scheduled to be chief of the technical division of the Point IV Program which would spend millions of American dollars in underdeveloped areas of the world. A recent phone call to the State Department revealed that Hanson's current position is Acting Assistant Administrator of the Point IV Program.

The Tydings Report gave Hanson a complete clearance.

Louis Budenz, former editor of the *Daily Worker* and the government's top witness in the trial of the 11 Communist leaders, testified before the Tydings Committee on the Hanson case. Budenz' sworn testimony was that Haldore Hanson was a member of the Communist Party.

Here is some of the evidence which I presented to the Tydings Committee on Haldore Hanson.

Evidence of Communist Subversion

When the Japanese-Chinese war broke out in China, this young man in partnership with Nym Wales, wife of Edgar Snow—both of whom have been named under oath as Communists—was running a Communist-line magazine in Peiping, China. He spent several years with the Communist Armies in China writing stories and taking pictures which the Chinese Communists helped him smuggle out of the country.

After his return from China, Hanson wrote a book— *Humane Endeavor.* On page 349 of his book Hanson condemns the anti-Communist groups in the Chinese Government for "Fighting against the Democratic Revolution as proposed by Mao Tse-tung and the Communists."

Hanson points out on the same page, 349, that anti-Communist officials within the Chinese government were making indirect attacks upon the Communists and that: "leaders of the Communist Youth Corps were arrested by military officers at Hankow. I myself was the victim of one of these incidents and found that local officials were the instigators."

So, we find that this employee of the State Department has a record of arrest in China with leaders of the Communist Youth Corps.

On page 350 we find that Hanson's passport was seized by the police in Sian when they found that he was traveling from Communist guerrilla territory to the Communist headquarters. He states that: "The man responsible for this illegal action was Governor Ching Ting-wen, one of the most rabid anti-Red officials in China. The governor's purpose was merely to suppress news about the Communists."

Throughout the book Hanson shows that not only did he have complete confidence in the Communist leaders but also that they had complete confidence in him. On page 256 he tells how Communist generals Nie and Lu Chen-Tsao acted as his couriers smuggling packets of film and news stories for him with the aid of Communist guerrillas into Peiping. In this connection, it is significant that Hanson admits that the Communists do not tolerate anyone who is not completely on their side.

Hanson makes it very clear all through the book that he is not only on the side of the Chinese Communists but that he has the attitude of a hero worshipper for the Chinese Communist Generals.

His respect and liking for the Communist leaders permeates almost every chapter of his book. For example on page 284 and page 285, he tells about how some ragged waifs, whom he had gathered into his sleeping quarters, regarded as "gods" Mao Tse-tung, the leader of Communist China, and Chu Teh, heir of Soviet Agent Smedley's estate and the Commander-in-Chief of the Chinese Red Armies now fighting us in Korea. He follows the system used in Lattimore's books of praising the Communists, not in his own words but in the words of some nameless waif who, of course, is anonymous.

A government job is a privilege, not a right. There is no reason why men who chum with Communists, who refuse to turn their backs upon traitors . . . should be given positions of power in government.

Hanson says on page 303 that Communist China's leaders "impressed me as a group of hard-headed, straight-shooting realists."

After an interview with Mao Tse-tung, leader of Red China, he states: "I left with the feeling that he [Mao Tse-tung] was the least pretentious man in Yenan and the most admired. He is a completely selfless man."

Following is Hanson's description of how the Communists took over China. I quote from page 102:

Whenever a village was occupied for the first time, the

Reds arrested the landlords and tax collectors and held a public tribunal, executed a few and intimidated the others, then redistributed the land as fairly as possible.

In connection with Hanson's position as acting assistant director of the Point IV Program, the following on pages 312 and 313 of his book would seem especially significant. He quotes Mao Tse-tung, the Communist leader, as follows: "China cannot reconstruct its industry and commerce without the aid of British and American capital."

Following are my concluding remarks about Haldore Hanson before the Tydings Committee:

> Can there be much doubt as to whether the Communist or the anti-Communist forces in Asia will receive aid under the Point-Four Program with Hanson in charge?

> Gentlemen, here is a man with a mission—a man whose energy and intelligence, coupled with a burning all-consuming mission, has raised him by his own bootstraps from a penniless operator of a Communist magazine in Peiping in the middle thirties, to one of the architects of our foreign policy in the State Department today—a man who, according to State Department announcement No. 41, will be largely in charge of the spending of hundreds of millions of dollars in such areas of the world and for such purposes as he himself decides.

> Gentlemen, if Secretary [of State Dean] Acheson gets away with his plan to put this man, to a great extent, in charge of the proposed Point-Four Program, it will, in my opinion, lend tremendous impetus to the tempo at which Communism is engulfing the world.

> On page 32 of his book, Hanson apparently tries to justify "the Chinese Communists chopping off the heads of landlords—all of which is true," because of "hungry farmers." That the farmers are still hungry after the landlords' heads have been removed apparently never occurred to him.

> On page 31 he explained that it took him some time to appreciate the "appalling problems which the Chinese Communists were attempting to solve."

Secretary Acheson is now putting Hanson in a position in which he can help the Communists solve the "appalling problems" in other areas of the world with hundreds of millions of American dollars.

Guilt by Association

Is not a person presumed innocent until proven guilty?

Yes.

Why do you condemn people like [Dean] Acheson, [Philip] Jessup, [Owen] Lattimore, [John] Service, [John Carter] Vincent and others who have never been convicted of any crime?

The fact that these people have not been convicted of treason or of violating some of our espionage laws is no more a valid argument that they are fit to represent this country in its fight against Communism than the argument that a person who has a reputation of consorting with criminals, hoodlums, gamblers, and kidnappers is fit to act as your baby sitter, because he has never been convicted of a crime.

A government job is a privilege, not a right. There is no reason why men who chum with Communists, who refuse to turn their backs upon traitors and who are consistently found at the time and place where disaster strikes America and success comes to international Communism, should be given positions of power in government.

What is your answer to the charge that you employ the theory of guilt by association?

This should properly be labeled *BAD SECURITY RISK BY ASSOCIATION* or *GUILT BY COLLABORATION* rather than *GUILT BY ASSOCIATION*.

The State Department, whose publicity agents complain the loudest about guilt by association, has adopted in their loyalty yardstick what they condemn as the theory of guilt by association.

For example, one of the categories of people they have declared unfit for service in the State Department is: "A person who has habitual or close association with persons known or believed to be in categories A or B." (Defined as a Communist or one "serving the interests of another government in preference to the interests of the United States.")

In this connection I might add that the State Department's loyalty and security yardstick is all right. The trouble is that they do not use that yardstick when the loyalty measurements are made.

In upholding the constitutionality of the Feinberg Law, the purpose of which was to weed Communists out of teaching jobs in New York, the United States Supreme Court said:

> One's associates, past and present, as well as one's conduct, may properly be considered in determining fitness and loyalty . . .

> From time immemorial, one's reputation has been determined in part by the company he keeps . . .

> We know of no rule, constitutional or otherwise, that prevents the state when determining . . . fitness and loyalty of . . . persons, from considering the organizations and persons with whom they associate.

In passing upon the constitutionality of that part of the Taft-Hartley Law which requires a non-Communist oath, the Supreme Court said:

> The conspiracy principle has traditionally been employed to protect society against all "ganging-up" or concerted action in violation of its laws. No term passes that the Court does not sustain convictions based on that doctrine for violations of the anti-trust laws or other statutes. However, there has recently entered the dialectic of politics a cliche used to condemn application of the conspiracy principle to Communists.

> "Guilt by Association" is an epithet frequently used and little explained, except that it is generally accompanied by another slogan, "guilt is personal." Of course it is; but personal guilt may be incurred by joining a conspiracy. That act of association makes one responsible for acts of others committed in pursuance of the association.

I have not urged that those whom I have named be put in jail. Once they are exposed so the American people know what they are, they can do but little damage.

As J. Edgar Hoover said before the House Un-American Activities Committee: "Victory will be assured once Communists are identified and exposed, because the public will take the first step of quarantining them so they can do no harm."

Strangely enough, those who scream the loudest about what they call guilt by association are the first to endorse innocence by association.

For example, those who object most strongly to my showing Jessup's affinity for Communist causes, the Communist money used to support the publication over which he had control, and his close friendship and defense of a Communist spy, also argue Hiss' innocence-by-association. The argument is that Hiss was innocent because Justices [Felix] Frankfurter and [Stanley] Reed testified they were friends of his, because Acheson chummed and walked with him each morning, because Hiss was the top planner at the United Nations conference and helped to draft the Yalta agreement.

We are not concerned with GUILT by association because here we are not concerned with convicting any individual of any crime. We are concerned with the question of whether the individual who associates with those who are trying to destroy this nation, should be admitted to the high councils of those planning the policies of this nation; whether they should be given access to top secret material to which even Senators and Congressmen are not given access.

The best analogy perhaps is the case of the applicant for a job as bank cashier who travels with safe crackers, robbers, and gamblers. Naturally, such a man would not be hired as cashier and allowed access to depositors' money. The fact that the bank president does not give him a job as cashier does not mean the job applicant has been found guilty of any crime. It merely means that the bank president, using good common horse-sense, decides that his depositors are entitled to have this man kept away from their money while he has associates who are bank robbers and safe crackers. Certainly in dealing with the lives of countless sons of American mothers and the liberty of 150 million American people, we should be using the same good common horse-sense that the bank president uses.

4

McCarthy's Methods Were Justified

William F. Buckley Jr. and L. Brent Bozell

Authors William F. Buckley Jr., the founder and editor of the *National Review*, and L. Brent Bozell, also once an editor of the periodical, are among the most well-known McCarthy defenders. In this essay Buckley and Bozell consider McCarthy's smear tactic, which the senator would employ by leveling serious and outrageous charges that, even if unsubstantiated, would sometimes result in ruining the target's career. Unlike many who criticize this favorite tactic of the senator's, Buckley and Bozell assert that, at least some of the time, McCarthy's smears were justified. However, his capacity to exaggerate damaged his own image and reputation as well as the validity of his own case. According to the authors, a case-by-case examination reveals that McCarthy should not be held accountable for character assassination in those instances where there was a solid basis for his charges. Ultimately, Buckley and Bozell insist that the senator's actions may be seen as justifiable since they brought a worthwhile degree of skepticism to the issue of security and loyalty.

I t is certainly not characteristic of McCarthy to come forward with dispassionate recitations of the facts. Rather, like an attorney summing up his case for the jury, McCarthy emerges as an *interpreter* of the fact: he assumes the role of the government advocate.

McCarthy, characteristically, seizes upon information that tends to point to disloyalty on the part of a government

Excerpted from *McCarthy and His Enemies: The Record and Its Meaning*, by William F. Buckley Jr. and L. Brent Bozell (Washington, DC: Regnery Publishing, 1954). Copyright © 1954 by William F. Buckley Jr. and L. Brent Bozell. Reprinted with permission.

employee, raises the broad issue of the employee's loyalty, and makes certain charges against the employee—i.e., he characterizes the employee as a "loyalty risk," as a "pro-Communist," as the "pioneer of the smear campaign against Chiang Kai-shek," or what have you. McCarthy's critics insist that it is a part of his method to do all these things without sufficient evidence to back him up. They insist, that is to say, that in almost every instance McCarthy has insufficient factual data, either to call into question the employee's loyalty, or to justify his particular characterization of the employee. Thus they conclude that he "smears innocent people."

We propose to survey McCarthy's record with a view to answering these two questions: Does the evidence he presents justify him (a) in raising the loyalty issue, and (b) in using the particular words that he uses in making his charges? . . .

McCarthy's Record

On the whole, McCarthy's attacks have followed a pattern. Most often he has gone after government employees, or former government employees. If the target of his attack is still employed, McCarthy calls for his dismissal. If he is no longer employed, he calls for an investigation of the security agency of the Department in which he worked. If he finds the employee has not even been processed (which is often the case), he lets the world know that he is flabbergasted. If he finds the employee has been processed and cleared (which is also often the case), he also lets the world know that he is flabbergasted.

McCarthy's critics have so effectively popularized the notion that McCarthy smears a half dozen Americans every week that the statistics may be surprising: the Grand Inquisitor of the Twentieth Century has publicly accused, as of questionable loyalty or reliability, a total of 46 persons. Of these 46, McCarthy mentioned twelve only once, and then only to point out that their security status was pending in the State Department and that eleven of them had nevertheless not been suspended from their work.

With respect to ten others, McCarthy merely quoted from derogatory reports developed by other investigators, with a view to persuading the Senate that at least a *prima facie* case existed for questioning the operating standards of a loyalty program that had cleared them. With one exception

(Remington), little public attention was given to these ten. They do not, in short, classify as "McCarthy cases" for purposes of shedding light on his method.

It is, consequently, on the basis of charges against twenty-four persons, whose cases he has especially dramatized, that McCarthy has earned his reputation as "a wholesale poisoner, a perverted destroyer of innocent reputations."

To get down to cases: McCarthy has never said anything more damaging about Lauchlin Currie, Gustavo Duran, Theodore Geiger, Mary Jane Keeney, Edward Posniak, Haldore Hanson, and John Carter Vincent, than that they are known to one or more responsible persons as having been members of the Communist Party, which is in each of these instances true. The fact that this charge against Hanson and Vincent is underwritten exclusively by Louis Budenz is not the basis of legitimate criticism of McCarthy; he cannot be called a smearer because he chooses to rely on the integrity of Budenz. Nor is McCarthy guilty of reckless character assassination because he chooses to take the word of the Spanish Government as against Gustavo Duran's; nor because he finds the testimony of the FBI undercover agents on Posniak's membership in the Party more persuasive than Posniak's denials. Mr. Robert Morris, assistant counsel for the Tydings Committee, offered to present to the Committee "some witnesses . . . who will testify that [Theodore Geiger] . . . was a member of the same Communist Party unit as they were.". . . Elizabeth Bentley has testified that Lauchlin Currie was a member of a Soviet apparatus. Mary Jane Keeney, having been named as acting as a Communist courier, was dismissed from her post with the United Nations after adverse loyalty reports on her were submitted by the State Department, and has since been cited for contempt by the Internal Security Committee of the Senate.

In short, McCarthy cannot, in our opinion, be indicted as a character assassin for circulating the above facts and for turning them into an accusation against the person concerned. And it readily follows that, in the light of such data, he was fully entitled to call their loyalty into question.

Is Smearing Justified?

[Owen] Lattimore has been identified as a member of the Communist Party by Louis Budenz, and as a member of

Russian Military Intelligence by Alexander Barmine; and the McCarran Committee classified him, in a unanimous report, as a "conscious articulate instrument of the Soviet conspiracy." There can be no denying, then, that McCarthy was justified in calling Lattimore's loyalty into question.

But McCarthy's specific charges against Lattimore went a good deal further than publication of the evidence that was available; and for this exaggeration he is indeed censurable. He told the Tydings Committee (in executive session, to be sure) that Lattimore was the "top Soviet espionage agent in America"—a daring allegation in the light of our notorious ignorance of the hierarchy of the Soviet espionage apparatus. A few days later, McCarthy modified this charge, in a speech from the Senate floor.

(It was not McCarthy, one must remember, who publicized Lattimore as the "top American espionage agent"; [columnist] Drew Pearson broke the story that McCarthy had so described Lattimore in a *closed* session of the Tydings Committee. It was thus a friend and admirer of Lattimore who set in motion Lattimore's "ordeal by slander.")

McCarthy cannot, in our opinion, be indicted as a character assassin for circulating . . . facts and for turning them into an accusation against the person concerned.

Though McCarthy's exaggeration is deplorable, it can hardly be maintained that it has been responsible for severely damaging Lattimore. Our society (as distinct from our laws) does not appear to attach much importance to the distinction between membership in the Party, and espionage in behalf of the Party. . . .

To return to the instances in which McCarthy did *not* misinterpret or exaggerate: McCarthy's insistence that John Stewart Service was a loyalty risk is supported in every respect. Service *was* named by General Hurley as a member of the State Department cabal that was attempting to undermine Hurley's influence in China and urging a policy essentially pro-Chinese-Communist. And Service *was* arrested by the FBI on charges of releasing classified material to unauthorized persons. Nor is that all: the Civil Service Loyalty

Review Board ultimately concurred in McCarthy's judgment—to the extent, at least, of ruling that there was a "reasonable doubt" as to Service's loyalty.

Thus it cannot be said that McCarthy smeared Service either in the way he framed the charges against him or in the fact that he called into question Service's loyalty. . . .

Of William T. Stone, McCarthy has said that his "Communist activities are legion.". . . An extremely cautious man might have said "dubious" instead of "Communist." But let us remember that the State Department security office, after studying Stone's record as far back as March, 1946, had recommended that "action be instituted to terminate his services with the State Department immediately." Held to strictest account for the phraseology of his charge, McCarthy probably "smeared" Stone; but if he did, he smeared a man who through the years had taken little pains to protect himself from such charges as were levelled against him. As for the second question we are asking (was McCarthy entitled to call Stone's loyalty into question?), the Department security division's own recommendation provides the obvious answer: Yes.

John Paton Davies has been a target of McCarthy ever since 1950. McCarthy quoted General Hurley as having accused Davies of encouraging, behind his back, a policy favorable to the Chinese Communists. "Davies has been suitably rewarded by Dean Acheson for his sell-out of an ally," said McCarthy to the Senate. "Davies [is now] . . . in Washington as a member of the State Department's Policy Planning Committee, where he is strategically placed to help further the betrayal he began in Chungking." Hard talk, certainly. But "betrayal" is a word that American political lingo was using generously long before McCarthy appeared; and we cannot demand of McCarthy greater verbal precision than is considered par in his métier. But we must not beg the question: McCarthy unquestionably considers Davies a security risk. He is at least not alone in questioning Davies' reliability; the McCarran Committee found that Davies "testified falsely" on a matter "substantial in import" (i.e., concerning his alleged recommendations that the CIA retain certain persons known to be Communists). We do not believe, therefore, that either McCarthy's specific charges against Davies or his calling Davies' loyalty into question were unreasonable. . . .

Summarizing the security file on Peveril Meigs, Mc-Carthy said in February, 1950, "So far as I know, everything in this individual's file indicates that he is actively working with and for the Communists." Whether this is so, and therefore whether McCarthy is guilty of having smeared Meigs, we do not know, not having had access to the file in question. It is public knowledge, however, that subsequent to McCarthy's charges against Meigs, he was discharged from the Army under the loyalty program. Therefore, the presumption is that McCarthy's questioning of Meigs' loyalty was reasonable.

Drew Pearson definitely *was* smeared by McCarthy on both counts; and the only defense McCarthy could possibly make (which we do not propose to encourage) would run in such terms as, "Those who live by the smear shall perish by the smear." (Pearson's case is treated in another section of this chapter, where it is particularly relevant.)

This, then, is McCarthy's record. As regards one of the two fundamental questions we have been asking (are Mc-Carthy's specific charges warranted in the light of his evidence?), it is clear that he has been guilty of a number of exaggerations, some of them reckless; and perhaps some of them have unjustly damaged the persons concerned beyond the mere questioning of their loyalty. For these transgressions we have neither the desire to defend him nor the means to do so. Measured against the moral command that proscribes every witting divergence from the truth, they are reprehensible. It remains only to be said that *McCarthy's record is nevertheless not only much better than his critics allege but, given his métier, extremely good.*

The essence of McCarthy—and McCarthyism— lies then in bringing to the loyalty-security problem a kind of skepticism with which it had not been approached before.

As regards the other standard for determining whether smearing has been a characteristic of McCarthy's method (Does the evidence McCarthy presents justify calling into question his targets' loyalty?), the case-by-case breakdown clearly renders a verdict extremely favorable to McCarthy.

With the two exceptions of Drew Pearson and George Marshall, not a single person was accused by McCarthy whose loyalty could not be questioned on the basis of a most responsible reading of official records. And this is the only test that seems to be relevant for deciding whether McCarthy "habitually smears people." When a man's loyalty is questioned, more often than not it makes little difference to him just *how* and in what terms it is questioned.

We may be wrong. But if we *are* right in insisting that this is the apter test, then the record clearly exonerates McCarthy of "habitual character assassination" and of "smearing of innocent people."

Is McCarthy Guilty of Character Assassination?

"Character assassination" is, of course, a part of McCarthy's method only if we so choose to call the exposure of past activities and associations of government employees. McCarthy has tirelessly combed the records of public servants; and, when the evidence has warranted it, and Administration intransigence blocked other alternatives, he has publicly disclosed their past activities and associations and has raised the question whether, given their records, they merit public confidence. In this, McCarthy has served, so to speak, as a public prosecutor. His concern has not been with establishing "guilt," but with seeing to it that security personnel apply standards stringent enough to give this country the protection it needs against well-camouflaged Communists.

The role of public prosecutor is never an enviable one. His competence is usually judged, unfortunately, on the basis of the number of convictions he wins. The counterpart of the public prosecutor in the security field cannot hope for such clean-cut vindications. At most he succeeds in persuading the "jury"—the Loyalty Security Board—that the doubt as to Jones' loyalty or reliability is "reasonable." And even then, he must face the vituperation of those who not only deem the doubt *un*reasonable, but openly challenge the competence of *any* tribunal to adjudicate such a question.

Let us remember in this connection that it is never particularly difficult to offer a plausible explanation or defense for any stand—or association—that raises doubts as to loyalty or reliability. How often we find ourselves sympathizing, spontaneously and warmheartedly, with the witness who accounts for his participation in a Communist front in terms of a deeply felt identification with the humanitarian objectives with which that front was ostensibly concerned. And how often we fail to remind ourselves that, if the organization was in *fact* a Communist front, *somebody* concerned with it wasn't so much concerned with social reform as with furthering the interests of the Soviet Union, and that therefore the function of security agencies is precisely to look skeptically at explanations commonly accepted as plausible. The layman is perhaps entitled to accept the accounting of the front-joiner, and to despise the "morbid" suspiciousness of the person who does not accept it. But *not* the security agencies—and *not* a United States Senator who feels a vocation to see to it that they do their job. For the hard fact of the matter is that the suspicious person may be the wiser person. And because of bitter experience, we have adopted a national security policy which instructs security personnel to *be* suspicious, and to find against the individual if so much as a reasonable *doubt* exists as to his reliability. . . .

Notwithstanding the hectically promoted public impression, McCarthy does not make a practice of fabricating evidence. He does, however, make a practice of acting on the proposition—on which he insists the government also act—that Alger Hiss was not the last of the Soviet agents in our midst, and that Hiss' comrades do not publicly parade their allegiance to the Soviet Union.

Bringing Skepticism to the Loyalty-Security Problem

We have likened McCarthy's role to that of the prosecutor; but let us keep in mind the hazards of carrying the analogy too far. The greatest psychological propaganda victory the Communists and the Liberals have scored in this whole area has been to force everyone to discuss the loyalty-security issue in the terminology of law. The authors of this book are themselves guilty of having used, in the preceding pages, the organically inappropriate imagery of the law, because otherwise they could not join issue with the opposition. But it is palpably foolish to speak, in the area of government security, of "defendant" and "prosecutor," of "guilt" and "innocence," of "proof," of the "presumption of innocence," of the "right to confront one's accuser," of the "right to cross-examination," of "judgment by one's peers," and the rest of it.

So long as we continue to use this terminology we can hardly hope to understand the problem at hand, much less to cope with it. We have, in fact, understood and coped with it just to the extent that we have fought ourselves free, at some points, from the legal imagery and its misleading implications.

It is all to the good that we make the district attorney respect the rights of the accused and depend, for a verdict of "guilty," upon the unanimous approval of the jury. Only at our peril do we abandon such revered customs. But let us not be deceived by certain similarities between the role of a public prosecutor and the role of a McCarthy, or between the position of the accused in a murder trial and the position of a Vincent in a security proceeding. The differences between the two are far greater than the similarities, and they reflect all the wisdom we have acquired about how to deal with the Communists in our midst.

The essence of McCarthy—and McCarthyism—lies then in bringing to the loyalty-security problem a kind of skepticism with which it had not been approached before. Others took it for granted that Service backed the Chinese Communists and gave away classified material because he was fooled. McCarthy was prepared to suppose he did so because he was pro-Communist. . . . And he keeps on being skeptical: if, as so often happens, the evidence does not conclusively establish either hypothesis, McCarthy is there to insist that we cannot afford to *act* on any but the hypothesis that favors our national security. McCarthy would unquestionably admit that Service *might* be innocent; but he would never consent to reinstate him in a position of public trust.

This is the heart of McCarthy's method. It is in many respects as revolutionary as the Communist movement itself—and so it is unlikely to commend itself to people so short on knowledge, or even instincts, as to the nature and resources of the Soviet conspiracy as not to realize that we live in an unbrave new world, in which certain cherished habits of mind are not only inappropriate but suicidal. . . .

Much has been said about McCarthy's behavior in questioning James Wechsler of the New York *Post* in the course of an investigation of the State Department's overseas libraries. One of the charges against McCarthy that has arisen from this encounter—that McCarthy was seeking to intimidate the anti-McCarthy press—is pure nonsense; but a further charge—that McCarthy was advancing a basically unsupportable standard for testing a man's loyalty—has some superficial plausibility to it, and merits brief consideration. McCarthy told Wechsler:

> I feel that you have not broken with Communist ideals. I feel that you are serving them very, very actively. Whether you are doing it knowingly or not, that is in your own mind. . . .

> I have no knowledge as to whether you have a card in the party. . . . Your purported reformation does not convince me at all. I know if I were head of the Communist Party and I had Jim Wechsler come to Moscow and I discovered this bright man, apparently a good writer, I would say, "Mr. Wechsler, when you go back to the United States, you will state that you are breaking with the Communist Party, you will make general attacks against Communism, and then you will be our ringleader in trying to attack and destroy any man who tries to hurt and dig out the specific traitors who are hunting our [sic] country." You have followed that pattern.

McCarthy, it is alleged, is actually saying that if you support Communist objectives you are, obviously, a Communist, and if you attack them, this is a deceptive maneuver, and you are still a Communist—unless, of course, you subscribe to McCarthy's formula for attacking them.

If McCarthy had intended to set up such a standard as a general yardstick for weighing a man's loyalty, he would indeed have embarked on a venture in sheer insanity. For such a standard, with one or another modification, would indict as disloyal absolutely everyone who disagrees with McCarthy's brand of anti-Communism. Now McCarthy may sometimes be imprecise; but heaven knows he is no lunatic. It is only the observer who is determined *not* to understand McCarthy who, on considering the context in which the above statement was made, will go on to wrench such a meaning out of it. McCarthy was not, be it noted, talking about just *any* American; he was talking about James Wechsler, an admitted former Communist. He was laying down a standard one may or may not endorse, but one we have no business confusing with a standard for testing the bona fides of persons who do not have Communist backgrounds.

With respect to the Wechslers, McCarthy is saying two

things: (a) it is not unreasonable to suppose that Communist "renegades" who are now demonstrated *anti*-anti Communists, are pulling the wool over our eyes; for it is clearly conceivable that there are men around us who, for tactical reasons, have been instructed by the Party to feign conversion in order to attend more effectively to the Party's business; and (b) ex-Communists must therefore be looked at more skeptically than other persons when the question of their loyalty to the United States arises. They, McCarthy is saying, must prove their sincerity in a very particular sort of way—by doing their earnest best to expose the conspiracy of which they were a party; by disclosing, for example, the names of their former confederates. This is a special form of penance that McCarthy is in effect asking for. He may have gone too far, but he is reasonable in applying a standard *different* from that applicable to persons innocent of involvement in the Communist conspiracy.

5

The Relationship Between McCarthy and the FBI

The Federal Bureau of Investigation and Athan Theoharis

These memos from the Federal Bureau of Investigation were exchanged between FBI Director J. Edgar Hoover and his top assistants. They appear here with editorial comments from Athan Theoharis, a McCarthy scholar and historian. The memos reveal the FBI's collaboration in sharing information with Senator McCarthy. Within the series reprinted here, Hoover and his assistants reconsider their relationship with McCarthy. They express concern that the appointment of FBI special agent Frank Carr as chief of staff of McCarthy's committee will create the appearance of a direct "pipeline" of information from the bureau to McCarthy.

Memo, SAC [Special Agent in Charge] Washington Guy Hottel to FBI Director, September 19, 1950, FBI 121-41668-28

Former FBI Special Agent Don Surine, who is now employed as an investigator by U.S. Senator Joseph R. Mc-Carthy, . . . [requested] "a copy of the Bureau's summary report on [Owen] Lattimore.". . . Surine indicated that in the past, he had been able to secure some information from the New York Office of ONI [Office of Naval Intelligence]. He stated that he needed such a report inasmuch as Senator McCarthy, in the future, would not make any further allegations without being able to support such allegations by an

From *From the Secret Files of J. Edgar Hoover*, edited by Athan Theoharis (Chicago: Ivan R. Dee, 1991). Copyright © 1991 by Athan Theoharis. Reprinted with permission.

investigative report. He said that if he could get the report, he could attribute the information contained therein to another government investigative agency, explaining that "this is what happened in the Posniak Case.". . .

Surine said that if he had the Lattimore summary report, it would be handled in the same fashion as was done in the Posniak Case, explaining that he would insert the information appearing in the Bureau report in the form of a summary of information appearing in the CSC [Civil Service Commission] investigative files, thus making it appear that his office had secured a CSC file rather than a Bureau file. In this way, Surine said he would not be violating any laws inasmuch as the CSC summary report would not be a bona fide report of a government agency and thus a theft of government property case, as such could not be proved. He also believed that a theft of government property with respect to the information contained in the report could not be proved inasmuch as the information would be completely paraphrased making it impossible for any observer to determine that the information was actually taken from a Bureau report. . . .

[On February 21, 1950, Senator McCarthy had cited eighty-one cases of "known communists in the State Department," a charge that resulted in the establishment of a special Senate committee, chaired by Millard Tydings, to determine the validity of his charges. After completing its investigation, the Tydings Committee issued a report dismissing McCarthy's charges as unfounded. Responding in a Senate speech, McCarthy characterized the Tydings report as a "whitewash" and further claimed that the files which the committee had consulted to reach its conclusions had been "raped." To support this latter allegation, McCarthy cited the case of Edward Posniak, one of the eighty-one cases, and from a classified Civil Service Commission report he quoted information not included in the Tydings report on Posniak.

President Truman's 1948 executive order prohibited the release of any loyalty report to the Congress without the president's explicit authorization, so McCarthy could not have lawfully acquired the report on Posniak. Attorney General J. Howard McGrath therefore directed the FBI to initiate a criminal investigation to determine how McCarthy had acquired this "stolen property." McGrath's request placed the FBI in a bind and led Hoover and other

FBI officials to be extra-cautious in processing further Mc-Carthy requests for FBI assistance. The above memo describes the subterfuge by which FBI officials leaked information to McCarthy's staff.]

Memo, FBI Assistant Director D. Milton Ladd to Director, October 5, 1950, FBI 121-41668—Not Recorded

(1) To advise you that when Don Surine told us if we gave him a copy of the summary report on Lattimore, it would be handled in the same manner as was done in the Posniak case, he was undoubtedly unthinkingly referring to the document distributed by Senator McCarthy on July 25, 1950, which purported to be a Civil Service Commission summary of the investigation of Edward Posniak.

(2) To suggest we do not interview Surine concerning the above [as part of the investigation demanded by Attorney General McGrath as to how McCarthy had acquired a copy of the loyalty report on Posniak].

. . . You will recall on September 15, 1950, Surine . . . volunteered if he had the Lattimore summary report it would be handled in the same fashion as was done in the Posniak case. You noted, "Just what does he mean by this?"

You will recall that Senator McCarthy on July 25, 1950, made a statement on the floor of the Senate concerning "Mr. X" in the State Department, who was subsequently identified as Edward Posniak, subject to a full field loyalty investigation by the Bureau. In making his statement, Senator McCarthy distributed copies of a document which purported to be a Civil Service Commission summary of the investigation of Posniak. On July 25, 1950, the Attorney General asked us to conduct an investigation to determine the source from which Senator McCarthy obtained his document. The investigation disclosed that Senator McCarthy's document is apparently not an authentic copy of any document prepared by the CSC, the State Department or the Loyalty Review Board, according to representatives of these three Agencies. In addition, the document distributed by Senator McCarthy contains inaccuracies, and it was prepared in such a way as to indicate it could not have been prepared as a CSC summary of the investigation of Posniak. In addition, you will recall that on March 23, 1950, the [FBI's] Baltimore Office advised us that Surine had advised an Agent of that office that Senator McCarthy was going to expose Edward Posniak, a State Department employee. At that time, Surine had in his possession a memorandum, apparently from Senator Mc-Carthy's office, which included quoted material, apparently from Bureau investigative reports. The possibility exists that the document which Senator McCarthy used on July 25, 1950, is the same document which Surine had in his possession on March 20, 1950, and the possibility further exists that this is the document that Surine was referring to on September 15, 1950, as noted above. It would further appear from the above that Surine was not thinking when he said what he did on September 15, 1950.

If at any time the Committee came up with something having an FBI angle, the charge would be made that Carr was a pipeline.

At the suggestion of the Attorney General, I interviewed Senator McCarthy on August 4, 1950, as to the source of the document which accompanied his press release regarding Edward Posniak. Senator McCarthy refused to disclose his source, and he further said he had instructed the employees in his office not to disclose the source of any of his material, since he felt it his duty to protect his sources.

In view of the above, it is respectfully suggested that we do not interview Surine concerning his statement given to us on September 15, 1950. . . .

Memo, SAC Washington Guy Hottel to FBI Director, November 28, 1952, FBI 94-37708-76X

During a recent interview . . . Senator McCarthy indicated he anticipated closer cooperation with and more extended use of the FBI and its facilities following the beginning of the new Congress [the Republicans had won a sweeping victory in the 1952 elections, winning the presidency and control of both houses of Congress]. He said he realized that in the past it was not always to one's advantage to be seen talking to or associating with McCarthy, but that he felt all this would be changed now with his re-election and the new Congress.

Senator McCarthy . . . [plans] to confer with the Director in the not too distant future relative to obtaining suggestions for prospective investigative personnel for his investigative committee.

The above is being furnished for your information.

Memo, FBI Director J. Edgar Hoover to FBI Associate Director Clyde Tolson, December 1, 1952, FBI 94-37708-77

On November 28, 1952, Senator Joseph McCarthy called and stated he would become Chairman of the Senate Committee Investigating Government Operations and Expenditures. He stated he would be in need of a good staff and asked that I give some thought to recommending to him a number of competent investigators that he might consider for appointment to this staff. I would like to have this given prompt attention.

Memo, FBI Director J. Edgar Hoover to FBI Associate Director Clyde Tolson, January 13, 1953, FBI 94-37708-79X

Yesterday afternoon, Senator Joseph McCarthy called to see me. The Senator stated that he wanted me to feel free at any time to contact him whenever I saw any activity of any member of his staff on the new committees of which he will be chairman, which I did not feel was in the best interests of good administration.

The Senator discussed generally the over-all plans which he has for carrying on the work of his committee and will, no doubt, be in contact with us from time to time. . . .

Memo, FBI Director J. Edgar Hoover to FBI Assistant Directors Clyde Tolson, D. Milton Ladd, and Louis Nichols, March 18, 1953

Senator Joseph McCarthy called with reference to the [Charles Bohlen] appointment [as U.S. ambassador to the Soviet Union]. . . . He stated he was quite concerned regarding this entire picture as there was practically no change [in State Department loyalty procedures] and everything was running about the same as it was a year ago. Senator McCarthy wondered whether I could tell him in complete confidence just how bad [Bohlen] actually was. I told him this, of course, was very hard to evaluate; that we made the investigation and that the request for the investigation was not received by us until after [Bohlen] was named for the appointment. [One and one-half lines withheld on personal privacy grounds.]

[Three and one-half lines withheld on personal privacy grounds] I commented that I guessed it all depended on the viewpoint and how you looked at a thing of that kind; that quite a number of reputable persons spoke very highly of [Bohlen] and there were some people who had very detrimental things to say about him. Senator McCarthy asked whether I thought he was a homosexual and I told him I did not know; that that was a very hard thing to prove and the only way you could prove it was either by admission or by arrest and forfeiture of collateral. I stated this had not occurred in his case at all as far as we know, but it is a fact, and I believed very well known, that he is associating with individuals of that type . . . and certainly normally a person did not associate with individuals of that type. I stated he has been a very close buddy of [Charles Thayer] for many years and he is a well-known homosexual. The Senator was advised that we had no evidence to show any overt act, but he, [Bohlen], had certainly used very bad judgment in associating with homosexuals. The Senator stated this was a matter that he was almost precluded from discussing on the Floor [of the Senate]; that it was so easy to accuse a person of such acts but difficult to prove. I agreed and stated that it was often a charge used by persons who wanted to smear someone. . . .

The Senator referred again to [Bohlen's nomination] and stated he was going to make a talk on the Floor concerning [Bohlen] and he wondered if I had any public source information such as from the Daily Worker which he could use. I told him that we had investigated [Bohlen] from the security and morals angle and that frankly most of the material we got was from the State Department. I indicated we did not go into the analysis of political speeches, and so forth, as that was supposed to be handled by the State Department.

Memo, FBI Assistant Director Louis Nichols to FBI Associate Director Clyde Tolson, June 24, 1953, FBI 94-37708—Not Recorded

. . . [Senator McCarthy] thinks he has now made a lot of progress in building up the Committee Staff, that he is easing [Francis] Flanagan out and, in fact, is getting some Texas oil men to get up a job for Flanagan to get him out of the Committee completely.

He stated that he will make J.B. Matthews the Staff Director, that Matthews is very experienced, has a dominant personality and will be able to control the situation so far as the Committee is concerned, and he knows this will be highly pleasing to the Director.

It [sic] told the Senator that, quite frankly, while we had never expressed ourselved [sic] publicly, it was difficult for us to forget some of the activities of Mr. Matthews during the days of the Dies Committee [in the late 1930s when Matthews was counsel to that committee] when we were fighting with our backs to the wall, and further there had been instances wherein we had contacted Matthews and shortly thereafter seen items in the papers.

McCarthy was very much taken back by this and stated he had been led to believe by [three names withheld] that Matthews was very close to the Bureau and the Bureau held Matthews in high regard.

I told the Senator that we had never expressed ourselves on that point, that naturally we would subordinate our feelings on those fighting Communism but that he, McCarthy, should be cautious about Matthews issuing press releases. . . .

McCarthy said that he certainly was sorry to get this reaction and that he would be very cautious.

I do know that [name withheld] is very close to Matthews and Matthews, in fact, has been a bulwark for the anti-Communist writers in New York City. I think that we should give Matthews a chance and when he does take over as Staff Director, I think we should keep our guard up but at the same time, see if he has changed his ways.

[Hoover's handwritten notation: "Let me see what we have on Matthews first."]

[The Matthews appointment did not work out, but not because his interest in publicity threatened to compromise the FBI's covert assistance to McCarthy. The publication of an article by Matthews in the right-wing *American Mercury*, about communist influence among Protestant clergy, appeared almost concurrent with the announcement of his appointment as staff director and provoked a firestorm of criticism—heightened by McCarthy's Catholicism and his prominent support by Catholic church leaders. McCarthy was forced to seek Matthews's resignation. To resolve his recurring staff problem, McCarthy considered appointing an FBI supervisor, Frank Carr, as his new staff director.]

Memo, FBI Director J. Edgar Hoover to FBI Assistant Directors Clyde Tolson and Louis Nichols, July 14, 1953

Yesterday Miss Jean Kerr, formerly secretary [and currently administrative assistant] to Senator [Joseph] McCarthy, called to see me and stated that her visit was to be considered as confidential and that the Senator did not know that she was coming to see me. . . .

Miss Kerr . . . was considerably concerned about the situation existent in the Senator's Committee, growing out of the recent Matthews incident, and that she understood that there was a Special Agent by the name of Francis P. Carr attached to our New York Office that the Senator would appoint as Chief of Staff if I would agree to it but that I had not seen fit to accede to the request. She wanted to know whether I wouldn't reconsider this matter and either agree to the appointment of Special Agent Carr or suggest someone else who is either in the Bureau or has been in the Bureau who could be appointed to this position.

I told Miss Kerr . . . there was some misunderstanding as to my position in this matter. I stated it was not up to me to concur or not concur as to whom Senator McCarthy appointed as Chief of Staff of his Committee. I stated it was a fact that Senator McCarthy and Mr. Roy Cohn, counsel for the Committee, had been in contact with the Bureau and had inquired about the availability of Mr. Carr . . . [and] that Mr. Cohn had directly contacted Mr. Carr about this appointment. . . . I stated that the Senator and Mr. Cohn had been informed that I would not ask Mr. Carr to take the position as Chief of Staff of the McCarthy Committee and that I would neither approve nor disapprove if he took such a position, but it had been pointed out to the Senator that the appointment of an Agent now in the service and engaged upon work dealing with subversive activities would, no doubt, be seized upon by critics of the Senator and of the FBI as a deliberate effort to effect a direct "pipe line" into the FBI and that it would make it necessary for the Bureau to be far more circumspect in all of its dealings with the McCarthy Committee should Mr. Carr be appointed.

Miss Kerr . . . could see this aspect . . . and inquired as

to whether I would in any way indicate publicly that I disapproved of the Carr appointment should it be made. I told Miss Kerr that I would neither indicate approval nor disapproval of whatever Mr. Carr did should he resign from the Bureau.

She . . . was concerned that the Senator might make a very sudden decision as to the appointment for this position and she feared that he would either appoint Mr. [Robert] Kennedy . . . or assign [subcommittee general counsel Francis] Flanagan . . . to the position of Director of the Staff. She . . . believed that either of these designations would be unfortunate. I told her that I did not know anything about Mr. Kennedy but that I was pretty well familiar with . . . Flanagan and that certainly this Bureau could have no dealings with him, irrespective of what position he might hold.

She . . . hoped that the Senator might delay taking final action upon this matter and that I might give some thought to suggesting some name or names to the Senator as to what he should do or as to whom he should appoint.

She inquired . . . what I thought of Bob Lee who is now with the Appropriations Committee of the House. I told her that Mr. Lee had had a very good record in the Bureau and I believe he had been out of the Bureau long enough so as not to have anyone attach to any such appointment the same suspicion that would attach to an Agent now in the employ of the Bureau. I told her that the only ex-Agent I knew . . . without commitments in the immediate future was former Special Agent Robert Collier . . . but I did not believe he would be available for several months and I doubted whether he would be interested in the position now vacant with the McCarthy Committee.

Informal Memo, FBI Assistant Director Louis Nichols to FBI Associate Director Clyde Tolson, July 23, 1953, Nichols File

. . . [Senator McCarthy] is going to try to get [Deputy Attorney General] William Rogers to make available to the [Government Operations] Committee [which McCarthy chaired] instances wherein [Truman's Assistant Attorney General] James McInerney failed to initiate prosecutive action against subversives. He stated that no doubt there were numerous cases which McInerney squelched and that by investigating these cases, he would not be investigating anyone connected with the Eisenhower administration. I told McCarthy that I doubted if he could possibly expect to have any success inasmuch as his close associate [committee counsel] Francis Flanagan was very close to Mr. McInerney and likewise was close to Rogers. McCarthy then stated he had talked the matter over with [Vice President Richard] Nixon and Nixon thought it was a good idea. I then inquired if Flanagan was not also very close to Nixon. McCarthy stated they, of course, did know each other.

2. The Senator commented . . . that he now feels good over having former Special Agent Frank Carr on the staff and that he was very glad the Director finally approved Carr's coming with the staff. I inquired of the Senator if I understood him correctly, that it was his view that the Director had approved Carr's coming on the staff. The Senator stated that this was his understanding, that he had deliberately not contacted the Director as he wanted to be in the position of saying that he had not been in touch with the Director but that he had been led to believe the Director had approved Carr from comments from [his staff aides] Jeannie Kerr and Roy Cohn, in fact the Senator stated he had Jean Kerr see the Director as he wanted to avoid the position of talking to the Director.

[Hoover's handwritten insert: "No. I told Jean Kerr & Cohn I was opposed to it."]

I told the Senator I happened to be very familiar with the Director's position on Carr and the Director's position had never wavered from that which I had personally conveyed to him some weeks ago, namely, that we would not give Carr a leave of absence, we would not release him, we would not ask him to go to the Committee, we would not approve his going with the Committee, that obviously if Carr resigned and wanted to go with the Committee this was his business. I further told the Senator that I knew this was the position the Director had taken with Jeannie as well as Roy Cohn, that in essence the Director's position was that he would neither approve nor disapprove, that the Director had stated out of deference to him, the Senator, he would not make any public protest. . . .

I further told the Senator I expected the next time he saw the Director, the Director would literally and figuratively "give him hell."

I told the Senator that the appointment of Carr was bad

because it now placed a tight restriction upon the Bureau, that we would have to lean over backwards because if at any time the Committee came up with something having an FBI angle, the charge would be made that Carr was a pipeline and that it would have been so much better to have had an outsider. The Senator stated he understands this, that he hopes the Director will not be too angry.

I am wondering if it would not throw a little more consternation in the ranks if I would take Roy Cohn to task for telling the Senator the Director had approved Carr's going with the Committee.

[Tolson's handwritten insert: "I see no need to do this." Hoover's handwritten insert: "I agree with Tolson. Cohn will just doubletalk & fast."]

3. In the course of the conversation I told the Senator that we were worried for fear that the cause had suffered and that there was a very definite reaction setting in against Congressional Committees and he would be smart to get off on some other subject. The Senator stated he agreed, that he wanted to wind up the Voice of America situation, he had some good information on the effect that our stockpiling program was bad on American mines, namely, that we have been buying metals from foreign countries and have closed down our mines with the result that our mines are flooded, have not been kept up and are becoming worthless. . . .

4. In discussing information the Committee had on the smuggling of guns to Latin America, . . . I told the Senator I had to ask him directly for the information as we had previously asked Cohn, Cohn's secretary had referred the matter to Flanagan, Flanagan in turn had told us we could come down and review what information he had. I told the Senator quite frankly that we would not embarrass any Agent of this service by sending him to that "SOB" Flanagan to secure anything. The Senator personally got the file and gave it to me.

The Senator then stated that Flanagan was out of the way and was completely off in a corner and that he was arranging to get Flanagan the job as counsel for a shipping company in which Clint Murchison owns an interest . . . [having] adopted the practice with the staff of trying to take care of each staff member as a means of building loyalty. I told the Senator he was shadow boxing, that certainly Flanagan was not loyal to him and that he ran the risk of having Flanagan alienate his chief financial support [Texas oil millionaire Clint Murchison]. I don't know how much effect this had on the Senator.

Memo, FBI Executives' Conference to FBI Director, October 14, 1953, FBI 121-23278—Not Recorded

The FBI Executives' Conference . . . considered current policy relative to furnishing information from Bureau files outside of the Executive Departments and made recommendations as to future procedures. As the problem covers a wide area, it is broken down, as set forth below, under separate captions. . . .

DISSEMINATION OF INFORMATION TO CONGRESSIONAL COMMITTEES:

. . . We have furnished information to the Senate Permanent Investigating [sic, Investigations] Committee (McCarthy) up until the late Summer [1953] when the Committee appointed [former FBI supervisor] Frank Carr as Staff Director. Since then no information has been furnished to this Committee. . . .

Chapter 2

Assessing McCarthy and McCarthyism

1

McCarthy Was a Fanatic

Michael Straight

Michael Straight became a writer and editor for the *New Republic* after serving in several government posts. He worked in the State Department, in the Department of the Interior, as secretary to the Emergency Committee of Atomic Scientists, and as chairman of the American Veterans Committee. This excerpt from Straight's 1954 book, *Trial by Television*, describes McCarthy's testimony before his own committee during the Army-McCarthy hearings, which had taken place earlier that year. According to Straight, an analysis of McCarthy demonstrates that he fits the profile of a fanatic, a theory that illuminates the senator's controversial techniques and outrageous claims during the investigations.

It was late on the thirtieth day of the [Army-McCarthy] hearings that Joseph McCarthy came to the witness chair. He was flanked as usual by Roy Cohn and Francis Carr. Across the room a large colored map was hoisted onto stands in preparation for a lecture on the Communist Party.

[Subcommittee counsel Ray] Jenkins had waited long for this proud moment. It was his misfortune that it followed hard after a ghastly hour in which McCarthy had tormented [army special counsel] Joseph Welch. In the revulsion that followed, Jenkins' carefully prepared questions, which would have seemed obsequious on the kindest of occasions, became so fawning that even the witness recoiled.

"What has been your interest in Communists, espionage, subversives, poor security risks?" inquired the special counsel. Senator McCarthy affirmed that he was disturbed by them. "Your position on Communism then, I take it, is well known, Senator?" "I think so," said McCarthy with a grin.

JENKINS. Your viewpoint, you would say, and their viewpoint are diametrically opposed to each other?

McCARTHY. That is right.

McCARTHY. You are not one of their fair-haired boys?

McCARTHY. You are right.

JENKINS. You have never been tendered their nomination by the Communist Party for the Presidency—is that what you mean?

McCARTHY. Not yet.

A low groan passed through the audience. Mr. Jenkins asked the Senator to tell the American public "just what the set-up of the Communists is." McCarthy heaved himself up with a sigh and crossed the room to the maps. As he spoke, he rapped upon them with a cane sent from Texas, with a handle carved in the shape of a longhorn steer. The map was brightly colored, and the names and addresses of Communist leaders were listed for each state save Texas, where the local patriotism of the oil men forbade any such slur. Some of these Communist leaders were dead; some others had long since left the party. One address in the South proved to be the property of a loyal box-holder who protested loudly. But the Senator could hardly be blamed if his material was not up to date. It was a perfectly good lecture whose weakest point was the admission that Communist strength had been halved in the final years of the Truman administration. But the Senator, who needed the Communists as the shark-sucker needs the shark, did not allow himself to be comforted by this development.

Senator McCarthy's Argument

The implication of Senator McCarthy's argument, unaccompanied by a broader perspective, appeared to be that by cleaning Reds out of Washington the American people could somehow exorcise the mounting dangers in the rice paddies of Indo-China, the villages of Southern India, the slums of Italy and France, the black ghettos of Africa, the schools and factories of Communist China and Russia.

And yet, while McCarthy ignored these mounting dangers, he foresaw nothing but war. "There are many people who think that we can live side by side with Communists," he told Jenkins. And when the counsel asked, "What do you say about that, sir?" he answered:

> MCCARTHY. Mr. Jenkins, . . . there is not the remotest possibility of this war which we are in today, and it is a war . . . ending except by victory or by death for this civilization.

The day faded; the hands of the clock wound around. Jenkins became restive.

> JENKINS. Senator McCarthy, . . . it is about closing time. . . . Now, while you have an audience of perhaps twenty or thirty million Americans . . . I want you to tell . . . what each individual American, man, woman and child can do . . . to do their bit to liquidate the Communistic Party.

The Senator nodded. First, he said, "They must depend upon those of us whom they send down here to man the watchtowers of the nation. . . ." Thus he assumed the whole executive role. Next he warned about teachers in schools, not the liberals or radicals, he added, but the real subversives. Lastly he called upon the voters to defeat all candidates for election who felt (with the President) that we should help allies even if they traded with China. Well satisfied, the special counsel reached for a perfect synthesis. What of "the hearthstone of the home" he inquired; was not that the place "to begin the inculcation into the minds of the youth of this nation . . . when the minds are young and pliable and impressionable?" Yes, said the witness, and the counsel went on to bring the Rotarians, the Optimists, the Kiwanis, the churches, the kindergartens, schools, and universities into his expanding vision of a nation where all citizens would pass through a McCarthy-made mold and be stamped "loyal."

In the days that followed, Jenkins developed his direct examination. Then he turned to cross-examination, begging the Senator's forgiveness. The Senator granted it, and Jenkins said nothing could make him happier than that. Once again he traced with McCarthy the familiar story that by now was boring and tedious. The Senator's testimony was interesting chiefly in that he also greatly softened his version of the crimes committed by John Adams and Robert Stevens. For example, on that old charge in the McCarthy brief, that Stevens and Adams "offered up the Navy, the Air Force and the defense establishment as substitute targets" and offered further to provide the "dirt," this exchange took place.

> JENKINS. . . . what precisely, Senator, did the Secretary and Mr. Adams say?
>
> McCARTHY. Again, Mr. Jenkins, I can't give you verbatim language. But they indicated that they were unhappy about any concentration on the Army; they indicated that if there was infiltration in the Army there must be in the Navy and Air Corps; and as I recall I heard Mr. Adams offer Mr. Cohn information in regard to the Navy. Just what language he used I don't know.

A strange concession for a man who had cried "Bribery" and "Blackmail"! So the testimony went, with almost every answer stopping short of the clear denial of what Army witnesses had said that could be turned over to the Department of Justice as possible perjury. Jenkins did establish to the satisfaction of everyone but McCarthy and his associates and close allies that improper pressures had been used on behalf of Private [David] Schine. It was necessary for the Senator to call General Reber and a great many other men "mistaken" in denying the charge. Eventually others joined in the questioning, but very little of significance developed. Welch seemed unable to decide whether he was back in the courtroom trying the legal core of the case, or still before the cameras with the job of education only half finished. The Democrats, who could not consult with Stevens or Adams each day, and had no files to work from, could not do Welch's job. In addition, beyond the incapacity of the panel of questioners, it was true that Senator McCarthy was less important than Roy Cohn in the case. Most important of all, the men around the table were by now nodding in weariness.

McCarthy Revealed by the Hearings

So the end of the hearings approached at last, and in the audience the question was voiced: What finally was accomplished by it all? No issues had been resolved, no allegation proved beyond doubt, no verdict established. Perhaps the phrase that would endure as the most accurate appraisal was spoken by [Senator] Stuart Symington when in one sharp exchange he said to McCarthy: "The American people have had a look at you for six weeks. . . ."

What had they seen?

McCarthy had shown, first, great physical strength and stamina. He had been more active than all other Senators put together in the hearings. He had gone off each weekend to campaign in Wisconsin. Yet rarely had his eyes closed and his head sunk on his chest in tiredness. He seemed in some obscure way to need the tension that others shunned, to feed on the conflict that exhausted his opponents, to draw nourishment from inflicting punishment and even from being hated and feared.

First was McCarthy's freedom from all rules and restraints, his total disregard for the ancient rule: Judge others as you would be judged.

He had shown great skill and resourcefulness as a showman and a fighter. He had created revulsion against the hearings and then turned it to his own use in demanding a halt to the show. He had driven the inquiry into the swamps and forests of side issues—and then denounced it as a waste of time. He had missed few opportunities to twist a phrase or turn a man's own thoughts against himself. When Ray Jenkins asserted that the soldiers at Fort Dix were packed like cattle in trucks, McCarthy protested in the name of American motherhood. When it developed without warning that Private Schine had been meeting in the evenings with the McCarthy subcommittee staff, McCarthy unhesitatingly launched an attack on the Army for shadowing the citizens of this free nation. His enormous charts were paid for by taxes; but when Jenkins produced a two-by-four photostat of Private Schine's telephone calls, McCarthy swore that he would start a special investigation into the sums poured into charts by the executive branch of the government.

He had shown charm on occasion; he had even shown humor. When he tried to ridicule by overstatement the privileges granted to Private Schine, his eerie snicker was the only sound in the silence of the Caucus Room. When he offered to provide some tobacco to replace Mundt's cigar his humor was pleasant, in the best Kiwanis Club tradition.

He showed a warmth and a desire to be liked, even by his opponents, which this reporter found almost touching.

Yet all this was the outward and peripheral Joseph McCarthy. Far more important were two revelations of his inner being.

First was McCarthy's freedom from all rules and restraints, his total disregard for the ancient rule: Judge others as you would be judged. Typical was his outrage at the "smears" against his staff even as he introduced smear after smear against Samuel Reber, Frederick Fisher, Theodore Kaghan, scores of men with no remote connection to the dispute.

Second was McCarthy's extraordinary power in pursuit of his immediate purpose; his single-minded concentration on gaining his objective regardless of the cost to others or to himself; his capacity to return again and again and again to his original contention and to refuse to yield it or to modify it, no matter how strongly attacked or how completely demolished it might be.

Those who watched McCarthy noted these obsessive qualities and tried to assess them in the conventional terms of cynicism and ambition, the emotions of ordinary men. Their efforts were futile, for McCarthy was no ordinary man. He was the product neither of Wisconsin, nor of any other community or communal experience. He was the unique phenomenon that occurs once in a hundred years.

McCarthy is not to be judged by our recognizable past. He is a forerunner and prophet of the American Brotherhood of the Guiltless. Like his brothers, his motivation must stem in part from the knowledge that he is steeped in conventional guilt. He leads the assault upon convention, hurling at society the very accusations which it would level at him. This is the capacity which leaves a nation bewildered as it appraises him by its own standards and symbols— which for him exist only to be abused.

It was Mr. Welch who expressed something of this reaction when he turned to the Senator during an executive session.

WELCH. Looking at you, Senator McCarthy, you have I think something of a genius for creating confusion . . . creating a turmoil in the hearts and minds of this country.

Joseph McCarthy has a genius for creating turmoil in the hearts and minds of this country, and the reason may be that turmoil has long raged in his own mind and heart.

The Profile of a Fanatic

The mind and heart in turmoil were well described by Eric Hoffer in *The True Believer*. "Only the individual who has come to terms with his self," writes Hoffer, "can have a dispassionate attitude toward the world. Once the harmony with the self is upset and a man is impelled to reject, renounce, distrust or forget his self he turns into a highly reactive entity." Hoffer continues:

> The fanatic is perpetually incomplete and insecure. He cannot generate self-assurance out of his individual resources—out of his rejected self—but finds it only by clinging passionately to whatever support he happens to embrace. This passionate attachment is the essence of his blind devotion and religiosity and he sees in it the source of all virtue and strength. . . . The fanatic is not really a stickler to principles. He embraces a cause not primarily because of its justness and holiness but because of his desperate need for something to hold on to. Often indeed it is his need for passionate attachment which turns every cause he embraces into a holy cause.
>
> The fanatic cannot be weaned away from his cause by an appeal to his reason or moral sense. He fears compromise and cannot be persuaded to qualify the certitude and righteousness of his holy cause. But he finds no difficulty in swinging suddenly and wildly from one holy cause to another. . . .
>
> Though they seem at opposite poles fanatics of all kinds are actually crowded together at one end. . . . They hate each other with the hatreds of brothers. They are as far apart and close together as Saul and Paul.

"The fanatic . . . finds no difficulty in swinging suddenly and wildly from one holy cause to another. . . ." In July 1949, a newcomer arose on the floor of the Senate to make a passionate defense of the belief that all men are innocent until proved guilty by due process of law. He denounced that group of nationalists who would "attempt to call up all the emotions of war and hatred." He scorned those who would "wave the flag and speak of the white crosses over the graves of the American dead." He condemned those who "ask in self-righteous phrases why . . . the government of the United States of America should concern itself with applying decent rules of justice to vicious criminals." He cried:

> Mr. President, America came into Europe with clean hands. The people of the world had come to respect not only America's great military and economic power but also to respect and admire her conception of decency and fair play and above all her judicial system which gave to every man no matter how much in the minority his day in court. This vast wealth of good will which had been built up over the years is being dissipated by a few men of little minds who unfortunately, in the eyes of the world, represent the American people.

This enemy of McCarthyism was Joseph McCarthy, speaking in defense of the rights of German soldiers tried and sentenced for the Malmedy massacre.

The fanatic rejects objective truth in dedication to the truth of his own creation.

". . . passionate attachment," says Hoffer, is the essence of the fanatic's "blind devotion." McCarthy was not at first a fanatic in his beliefs. He came late and a stranger to the cause of anti-Communism. His mood, on returning to Wisconsin from Wheeling, West Virginia, where he began his anti-Communist crusade, was one of amazement and delight at the political diamond mine into which he had stumbled. He was not then a believer in any cause but McCarthy. But gradually he came to believe his tirades—or so it seems.

The fanatic is egocentric. And so McCarthy in the hearings saw all issues and conditions in terms of himself. In these hearings, as in other inquiries, witnesses protested that their loyalty should not be judged by the sole standard of whether they supported or opposed McCarthy. To McCarthy there was no other standard and could be none. If the chairman or anyone else turned away as he spoke, McCarthy was enraged; his every point of order was "extremely important." He wanted deeply to be liked by everyone, but he would rather be hated than ignored. His own hatred was

directed impartially to men of either party who threatened
to take from him the center of the stage.

The fanatic stands above the law and above duly constituted authority. He disdains authority, which supports the
society he rejects. He scorns the law as the instrument of the
order he is psychologically committed to overthrow. So Mc-
Carthy claimed that he, rather than the responsible officials
appointed by the President, spoke for the Army. He stated,
"I just will not abide by any secrecy directive of anyone."

The fanatic seeks to destroy real and imagined enemies
who stand in his way. The fanaticism of McCarthy stood
forth in his original brief of counter-charges. The Army
brief had attributed to him a minor and rather moderate
role. Like one preoccupied with his own persecution, Mc-
Carthy struck back. He uncovered "motive" in the suppos-
edly criminal acts of Mr. [Assistant Secretary of Defense] H.
Struve Hensel. Late in the hearings, when his brief had lain
for five weeks before the public, he conceded that he had no
evidence whatever linking Hensel to the Army report. He
had simply read the report, remembered old charges against
Hensel, and then "put two and two together." McCarthy
had cried that [Francis] Carr and [Roy] Cohn had been
"smeared." Yet Hensel swore that McCarthy had told him
on May 3 that in attacking him he was following the advice
an old farmhand, Indian Charlie, gave him: "If one was ever
approached by another person in a not completely friendly
fashion one should start kicking at the other person as fast
as possible below the belt until the other person was rendered helpless."

Truth and Morality for the Fanatic

The fanatic rejects objective truth in dedication to the truth
of his own creation. Eric Hoffer quotes the view of Pascal,
that self-contempt produces in man "the most unjust and
criminal passions imaginable for he conceives a mortal hatred against truth which blames him and convinces him of
his faults." McCarthy seemed to have a distaste for the dis-
cipline of truth. He said of Symington, for example, "The
only time I hear him raise his voice at this table is when we
appear to be hurting those that defend Communism." This
demonstrably false charge, like the claim that [John L.] Mc-
Clellan wished to jail him, was one of McCarthy's big lies. It
was indignantly repudiated; but, following the advice of his

teacher, McCarthy repeated it over and over and over until in many untrained minds a part of it stuck. He usually did not lie outright, but distorted the facts to leave an impression that was false.

To the fanatic, morality is defined as that which advances his own cause. McCarthy upbraided Symington for using what he called Communist methods. Yet his own methods were flagrantly expedient; H. Struve Hensel swore, and the Senator did not deny, that two of McCarthy's agents falsely told a woman that her daughter had been involved in a hit-and-run accident simply to learn her son-in-law's address.

The fanatics of the extreme left, the Communists, treat morality as a by-product of the capitalist class structure. McCarthy also appeared indifferent to society's code of moral conduct. He seemed insensitive to the suffering he inflicted on others. He was plainly surprised when Welch declined to embrace him on the day after his attack on Frederick Fisher. Only once during the hearings did McCarthy show a glimmer of conscience. "I fear," he said, "I may have done an injustice to Mr. Hensel and John Adams." But at no other time did he indicate that there could conceivably be any wrongdoing on his part.

In McCarthy's world, if he was incapable of immorality his enemies were not. The attack upon him by Senator [Ralph E.] Flanders was "vicious" and "dishonest." The witnesses who criticized him were "grossly dishonest." The monitoring of telephone calls (which he himself had practiced) was "the most dishonest and indecent thing I have heard in years." Over and over he begged Symington "in common decency, in common honesty" to testify, as McCarthy had done. He employed verbal moral symbols, but ignored much of the content of moral teaching. But perhaps the use of words like "indecent" and "vicious" rose also from realms beyond reason. They were the same words that others might use in condemning McCarthy—that some part of McCarthy might even use to condemn himself.

Day and night, McCarthy lunged at real and imagined enemies. Only one was beyond his reach—the enemy within. It lurked there throughout the hearings, striking swiftly and withdrawing like the tongue of a snake.

2

The Tydings Committee Hearings Were a Sham

Richard H. Rovere

In early February 1950, Senator Joseph McCarthy delivered a controversial speech in Wheeling, West Virginia, in which he announced that Communist Party members had infiltrated the State Department and that he had a list bearing the names of those individuals. The Senate formed the Tydings Committee to investigate McCarthy's charges. The Democrats were the majority party in the Senate at that time, so McCarthy, a Republican, was a minority member of the committee before which he presented his official charges. Over the next several months, the committee heard testimony from several people who had to defend against the Wisconsin senator's accusations of Communist affiliation and subversion. It was during the Tydings Committee hearings that McCarthy's smear tactics came into national view.

Richard H. Rovere, a reporter who covered many of the hearings and investigations of the McCarthy era, wrote this account of the events surrounding the Tydings Committee. Rovere describes how McCarthy was called as the first witness to testify. He also recounts the most famous case presented to the committee, that of Owen Lattimore, a well-respected professor at Johns Hopkins University. Although Lattimore was not an employee of the State Department, he found himself in the position of having to defend against the senator's outrageous charges. The official finding of the Tydings Committee was that McCarthy's charges were a "fraud and a hoax."

Excerpted from *Senator Joe McCarthy*, by Richard H. Rovere (New York: Harcourt, Brace, Jovanovich, 1959). Copyright © 1959 by Richard H. Rovere. Reprinted with permission.

On February 22, the Senate had, by unanimous resolution, instructed the Foreign Relations Committee, "or any duly authorized Subcommittee thereof," to "conduct a full and complete study and investigation as to whether persons who are disloyal to the United States are or have been employed by the Department of State." In time, this language was to be the cause of much misunderstanding and bitterness; it was said, and not merely by McCarthy and his friends, that the Subcommittee under Senator [Millard] Tydings had neglected to discharge its broad mandate and, instead, had investigated only the charges brought by McCarthy, who, of course, was not mentioned in the resolution. The mandate was broad; it had to be broad to serve as a warrant for looking into the charges he had made. But his charges were the sole occasion for the investigation. No other Senator was saying that the State Department harbored disloyal persons in large numbers. And by the time the Committee (it so overshadowed the parent body that its status as a subcommittee was lost sight of and it was commonly called the Tydings Committee) was set up, it had become clear that all McCarthy's information and misinformation had come from the files of investigations conducted by the House of Representatives in the preceding Congress. No less than four House committees had covered exactly the same ground and had found nothing that would lend any substance to what McCarthy was saying. On the contrary, the man who had headed the investigation for the Committee on Foreign Affairs, a Michigan Republican named Bartel Jonkman, had said on the House floor:

> ... before the Eightieth Congress adjourns, I want the members to know that there is one department in which the known or reasonably suspected subversives, Communists, fellow-travelers, sympathizers, and persons whose services are not for the best interests of the United States, have been swept out. That is the Department of State.

McCarthy Testifies

McCarthy, by his own telling, had taken off soon after February 20 for Arizona and the "ten saddle-sore days" with "Rillabelle, old Jim Sands, and Old Jack with the hounds." He was back by March 7 and ready to be sworn as the first

witness before the Tydings Committee. He arrived on time
with his burden, the briefcase that contained "the picture of
treason [that was] to shock the nations and occupy the headlines until Truman declared war in Korea," opened it, shuf-
fled its contents a bit, and read the first case on his list of 81
"card-carrying Communists" in the State Department—
Judge Dorothy Kenyon, a lady lawyer from New York, who
had never worked for the State Department or any other
agency of the federal government for as much as five minutes. She had held an honorific membership on the United
Nations Commission on the Status of Women and had sat
on the Municipal Court in New York City, but had otherwise exercised her civic-mindedness as a private citizen. An
indefatigable doer of good works, a tireless joiner of organizations professing worthy aims, she had amassed quite a
record for becoming involved in what turned out to be
Communist-front organizations, and she had amassed quite
a record for getting out of them. McCarthy spent a day and
a half talking about the organizations she had joined and no
time at all telling about those she had left.

---

*McCarthy enacted before the Tydings
Committee essentially the same travesty on
reason, logic, and evidence he had put on before
the Senate on February 20.*

From early March through early July, the Committee
sat, its members gravely taking testimony that was in time
to bulk up into 1,500 printed pages and more than a thousand of documentation. The very thought of it is now somehow chilling—one must look to philosophy for an explanation. "Men are mad so unavoidably," Pascal said, "that not
to be mad would constitute one a madman of another order
of madness." This was a necessary but certainly mad enter-
prise. Millard Tydings was chairman of the Senate Committee on the Armed Services. Brien McMahon, who
shared most of his burdens, was chairman of the Joint Congressional Committee on Atomic Energy. The Tydings
Committee constituted more than one-third of its parent
body, the Foreign Relations Committee. In early 1950,
there were very few groups of men on this planet whose re-

sponsibilities were heavier than those of these men. Whatever the United States did in the world—and it was then doing, or attempting to do, a great deal—had to have their consent and, constitutionally, was supposed to have benefited by their advice. Every season of this decade [the 1950s] has been one of crisis, and it is perhaps going a bit too far, and waxing a bit too solemn, to maintain that these months were uncommonly crucial. Yet it is no less than the truth that in those months we were grappling for the first time with the immense fact of the loss of China to Communism; that we were attempting to determine whether our commitment to Western Europe should be underwritten with large and permanent garrisons of American troops; and that we were making the first hydrogen bomb. In all these undertakings, the members of the Tydings Committee had an enormous role to play, yet the mad force of mad circumstances compelled them to sit and listen for days and weeks and months on end to a poolroom politician grandly seized with an urge to glory (and soybean futures) reciting facts that were not facts about State Department employees who were not State Department employees.

McCarthy enacted before the Tydings Committee essentially the same travesty on reason, logic, and evidence he had put on before the Senate on February 20—and was so often to put on in the coming months. Of course he had more time to fill. (He had told reporters that he planned to keep the hearings going into the autumn, so that they would be in the voters' minds on Election Day.) He spent four days testifying on ten people. Although he had said he was going to tell all about the 81 he had discussed in his February 20 speech (or the 66, when omissions and duplications were allowed for), these ten were added starters, as were 25 more he gave the Committee in closed session. He gave names but in nearly all cases no evidence. Where was the evidence? the Committee asked. In the State Department files, McCarthy would say. And Senator Tydings would point out that the resolution creating the investigation empowered the Committee to subpoena records only when charges had been made. "You have left the committee in a rather embarrassing position," Tydings once said. "How do we get the records? We are authorized to get them . . . if you or somebody makes a charge. [He meant, of course, a formal, specific "charge"—not the random accusations McCarthy was making every five minutes.] You say you are not making any charges." And McCarthy responded:

> I am not making charges. I am giving the committee information of individuals who appear by all the rules of common sense as being very bad security risks. . . . I am not in a position to file any formal charges. . . . If you want me to charge from the evidence . . .

But what evidence? It was all in the files. In exasperation, Tydings went to President Truman and implored him to let the Committee see the files, despite an executive order discontinuing the practice of releasing personnel files to Congressional committees and despite McCarthy's refusal to place any charges. The President agreed. Immediately, McCarthy called it "a phony offer of phony files." The records had been "raped and rifled," he said. The FBI information had been lifted from them. J. Edgar Hoover was asked to look the files over and see if this was true. He wrote to Tydings and said that "the State Department files were intact" when his staff, at the Committee's request, had inspected them.

The Lattimore Case

Twice, when McCarthy seemed to have strained the Committee's credulity to the point of danger to himself, he announced that he was going to rest everything on one big case—he would be willing, he said, to have the Committee call the whole show off and report him as a faker if the Committee was unimpressed by the evidence he had on a single person. On March 10, he said he would go for broke on the case of a man in "an important post" in the Department. He needed only the weekend to gather and organize the data; he would be ready first thing Monday morning, March 13.

He could not make time stand still. The morning came. McCarthy showed up, briefcase in hand. Rumpled and breathless, he explained to the Committee that he was all ready with his case, but that something terribly important had come up—a Senate debate on housing. He high-tailed it for the door. A committeeman hailed him back—saying that word had just come up that the housing debate had been postponed. That was good news, McCarthy said, for he had another pressing matter to attend to—some Wisconsin constituents had just come to town and were waiting in his office. He had to see them right away. But the Committee wouldn't let him go. It sat him down and asked for his evidence. He said he would be glad to give evidence and that he had, in fact, four cases he wished to present. One was in the Navy, two were in the State Department, and one, Owen Lattimore, was a professor at Johns Hopkins University.

McCarthy soon found a way of spicing his disquisitions with sex. He had discovered that homosexuality was regarded as a factor in security judgments.

The Lattimore case—the second one on which he was ready to go for broke, unless Lattimore was the first one as well—as probably the most celebrated of all his cases. He did not pursue it that morning of March 13. He merely said Lattimore was "an extremely bad security risk." But about a week later, he began telling the press that he was on the verge of naming "the top Russian espionage agent" in the United States. "I am willing to stand or fall on this one," he said. "If I am wrong on this, I think the Subcommittee would be justified in not taking my other cases too seriously." I have always been convinced that when he first talked about his "top espionage agent," he hadn't the slightest notion which unfortunate name on his list he would single out for this distinction. I also believe that he sensed almost immediately that he had made a rather foolish mistake in picking Lattimore. For although in the end he managed to create a good deal of doubt about Lattimore (who made some notable contributions of his own in the way of creating doubt about himself), he could hardly, at the time, have chosen worse. Lattimore wasn't a spy, he wasn't a State Department employee, and he wasn't a Communist— though at times, in the thirties and forties, he had been a stout fellow-traveler and an eloquent advocate of a view of Asia that accorded with the Communist view. He was a kind of academic and journalistic politician, and McCarthy was subsequently to stumble over a half- or quarter-truth when, having given up on the claim that Lattimore was a spy, he described Lattimore as "the chief architect of our Far Eastern policy." A generation of China hands in the State Department had read Lattimore for years and had been greatly influenced by his views.

But McCarthy had known nothing of this when he started out. He needed a spy to keep things lively in the Tydings Committee. Owen Lattimore was tapped. He was made the arch-arch-villain—"Alger Hiss's boss in the espionage ring in the State Department." McCarthy claimed he had witnesses queued up outside the Caucus Room to sustain this. A bedraggled collection of apostate Communists came in to say lamely that although Lattimore was not their beau ideal of an anti-Communist partisan, they lacked any shred of evidence that he was a Communist spy or even a Communist. "Maybe in the case of Lattimore I have placed too much stress on the question of whether or not he has been an espionage agent," McCarthy said. But he was a "policy risk" and an architect. "I believe you can ask almost any school child who the architect of our Far Eastern policy is, and he will say 'Owen Lattimore.'" I remember what comic relief the line brought to the press gallery when McCarthy produced it in a floor speech on March 30. But as that spring wore on, the statement acquired a validity—a time did come when, if McCarthy's question had been posed to schoolchildren, many would have given McCarthy's answer.

Attacking Homosexuality as a Security Risk

The whole affair was nasty and squalid and offered little in the way of comic relief. McCarthy debased the currency of discourse with bad and counterfeit tender, and Gresham's Law set in. And there was more nastiness. McCarthy soon found a way of spicing his disquisitions with sex. He had discovered that homosexuality was regarded as a factor in security judgments, and he worked this for what it was worth, which was quite a bit. It gave lesser demagogues, who realized that the Communists-in-government issue could never be taken from him, a corner of McCarthyism to work for themselves. A subcommittee of the District of Columbia Committee was set up to investigate "sexual deviates" (I believe this ugly phrase was invented at that time) in government. An early bulletin from this group told of reports it had of a Russian scheme to lure "women employees of the State Department under their control by enticing them into a life of Lesbianism." The District Police set up a special detail of the Vice Squad "to investigate links between homosexuality and Communism."

Guilt by Association

Nothing, though, was more embarrassing than the kind of replies McCarthy's victims felt themselves called upon to make. McCarthy accused them of being spies and Communists; if he was in error, it was, it seemed, their job simply to inform the Tydings Committee of this fact and to offer such evidence as they may have had that they were not. What many did was to supply wholly gratuitous information intended, apparently, to show McCarthy that they were men in possession of exactly the kind of virtues he should admire. It was not enough, in those days, for anyone to say that he wasn't a card-carrying Communist; many felt impelled to show that they were dues-paying Redmen or Epworth Leaguers or Lions. Haldore Hanson, an official of the State Department's Office of Technical Cooperation and Development, made public this chapter of his biography in his prepared statement before the Committee:

> I was active in the YMCA from the age of ten. I went to YMCA summer camps and was President of the Hi-Y Club during my high-school years. From the age of twelve, I was a Boy Scout. I became an Eagle Scout, a Boy Scout Camp Counsellor, and served as Scoutmaster during my first year of college. I was active in the Presbyterian Church, of which all my immediate family were members. My father was a Sunday School superintendent. During my senior year in high-school, I was awarded a summer in Europe as a result of an essay contest sponsored by a boys' magazine. . . . By means of scholarships, a job waiting on table, and loans, I was able to finish my college education. . . . I was elected to Phi Beta Kappa. . . . I was a debater and on the track squad.

In New York, at the height of it all, the Secretary of State addressed the American Society of Newspaper Editors and explained that "There is no need for anyone to be defensive about the Department of State." It was a splendid body of men, including such figures as "George McGhee, of Texas, a former oil man . . . Willard Thorp, a former partner of Dun & Bradstreet . . . Paul Nitze of Massachusetts, a former partner of Dillon, Read," and so on. Not only was the defense humiliating to those who employed it, but it raised the delicate question of what the large sections of the population who had never been Eagle Scouts and might even have been in the bad graces of Dun & Bradstreet would do if attacked by McCarthy. Moreover, some of the defenses could be used to establish guilt by association. The Communists had always found excellent pickings among Eagle Scouts and college debaters, and they had done tolerably well among persons with impeccable business and family connections. One of McCarthy's victims who never denied his Communist sympathies (though he was never in the State Department) was Frederick Vanderbilt Field, who could hardly have chosen more felicitous forebears. And Alger Hiss, a real Hi-Y sort, had been a debater, a track man, and the "best hand-shaker" in his class at Johns Hopkins.

A Clean Bill of Health for the State Department

The Tydings Committee issued an interim report in mid-July. Before he saw it, McCarthy said it would be a "disgrace to the Senate." He confirmed his prediction a few days later by calling it "a green light for the Reds." The report said that McCarthy had imposed a "fraud and a hoax" on the Senate: "Starting with nothing, Senator McCarthy plunged headlong forward, desperately seeking to develop some information which, colored with distortion and fanned by a blaze of bias, would forestall the day of reckoning." The two Republican members—[Henry Cabot] Lodge, of Massachusetts, and Bourke Hickenlooper, of Iowa—did not sign the report. They complained that the investigation had not been broad enough to warrant the issuance of a clean bill of health to the State Department, which was, in effect, what the majority report did.

3

The Senator's Support Weakened During the Army-McCarthy Hearings

Robert Griffith

One of the most expert of McCarthy scholars, Robert Griffith, provides an overview of the Army-McCarthy hearings. In these bizarre hearings before the Permanent Subcommittee on Investigations, McCarthy and his top adviser, Senate counsel Roy Cohn, questioned the loyalty of several army officers, most of whom worked out of Fort Monmouth. Many of McCarthy's critics saw the senator's attack as a personal vendetta against the branch of the military that had refused to provide an officer's commission to a young friend and aide of the senator's, G. David Schine, who was found unfit for commission by the army. These hearings, broadcast on television and radio, signaled the beginning of McCarthy's downfall. With his smear tactics on display before the entire nation, McCarthy earned the ire of President Eisenhower, a fellow Republican, and the Wisconsin senator soon found himself at odds with his own party, even within the Senate.

The army-McCarthy hearings sprawled out through nearly two months of confusion and turmoil. In a special sense they were a dramatization of all which had come to be associated with Joseph R. McCarthy. And yet their meaning remained cryptic and elusive. The issues, both real and contrived, were more often than not obscured and

Excerpted from *The Politics of Fear: Joseph R. McCarthy and the Senate*, by Robert Griffith (Amherst: University of Massachusetts Press, 1970). Copyright © 1970 by Robert Griffith. Reprinted by permission of the publisher.

muddied by the torrent of words poured forth during the hearings themselves.

Did Roy Cohn exert improper pressure in seeking preferential treatment for his friend and traveling companion, G. David Schine? The answer was yes. Cohn had been by turn arrogant, insulting, and abusive in his demands that Schine be given special favors, though Senator McCarthy's role in all of this was as much one of acquiescence as of actual connivance. Had the army sought to end McCarthy's investigations? The answer here too was yes, although not at all in the way McCarthy alleged. The idea that the United States Army was actively "coddling Communists" was absurd. If anything, the army had plunged overboard in the opposite direction. The secretary of the army was, in McCarthy's words, "a fine, naive, not-too-brilliant" Republican businessman who had tried to appease the senator and to deflect his energies elsewhere. Six months later these very acts of appeasement were exhibited by McCarthy as proof that the army was surely trying to hide something. No one questioned the primary assumption that McCarthy's "investigation" had been a valid attempt to guard the national security, and as a consequence the entire debate was delivered over into the realm of fantasy.

From the very beginning McCarthy dominated the hearings. He was a participant because of the charges made by and against him, a cross-examiner by virtue of the privileges won during the battle over procedures, and the center of continuing controversy by the sheer exercise of will with which he overpowered Chairman [Karl] Mundt and the other members of the subcommittee. McCarthy had always lacked a sense of inner restraint, and in the lax and permissive atmosphere of the Senate caucus room he roamed almost at will.

The Composition of the Mundt Subcommittee

The hearings proceeded awkwardly. Subcommittee counsel Ray Jenkins would first interrogate a witness on direct examination, then cross-examine him. The large-boned Tennessean was, despite a handsome criminal practice in his home state, ill equipped for the demands of his position. A more acute mind might have challenged the presuppositions of both McCarthy and the army. Jenkins was content to share in the collective unreality of the hearings and to lead the subcommittee into countless time-consuming digressions and superfluities.

More often than not, however, McCarthy's attacks were directed at the other participants in the hearings. His office had prepared dossiers on each person, and in the fire of battle the senator would use these charges, whatever their nature, to bludgeon his opponents.

When Jenkins had finished, the senators would direct their own questions to the witness. Each man was a study in the politics of the situation. Mundt, who had always supported McCarthy in the past and who was now up for re-election, was plainly unhappy with his duty. He had wanted neither the investigation nor the chairmanship which had been thrust upon him, and in the face of conflict he usually retreated into a cloud of midwestern geniality. [Everett] Dirksen was at his oratorical best, supporting McCarthy and yet trying to minimize and muffle the conflicts between the senator and the Republican administration. [Henry C.] Dworshak usually favored McCarthy also, although on occasion even he was harried by the senator's repeated "points of order." [Charles] Potter was the only Republican truly ambivalent toward McCarthy. Like [Robert C.] Hendrickson and other Republican moderates, he was a decent enough man, but he was torn between competing factional loyalties. As a freshman member of HUAC [the House Un-American Activities Committee] during the Eighty-third Congress he had won a reputation as "something of a junior McCarthy." In 1952 he had received aid from McCarthy in his narrowly successful campaign against Democratic incumbent Blair Moody. But he was also responsive to the demands of the administration, and at the end of the hearings this ambivalence proved an important factor in helping to check McCarthy.

The Democrats were cautious and circumspect. Each went to extreme lengths to establish his own *bona fides* as an anti-Communist, and not one of them directly challenged the assumption that McCarthy was a great Communist hunter. Still, they furnished the brunt of the opposition to McCarthy. Together with special army counsel Joseph L. Welch, they acted as the "prosecution," a role which inevitably led them into conflict with McCarthy.

John L. McClellan led the minority, and both Democrats and Republicans alike deferred to this wiry and unsmiling senior senator. He was restrained, judicious, even unimaginative, yet when he spoke it was with force and authority. [Henry] Jackson was moderate and direct, a good lawyer and an intelligent parliamentarian. But McCarthy's most intransigent foe on the subcommittee was Stuart Symington of Missouri. Symington remained doggedly in opposition throughout the hearings, and the clashes between the two men became increasingly bitter and violent. On June 4 the transcripts of the early March conversations between Symington and [Robert] Stevens were introduced into the record. "If you are going to play with McCarthy, you have to forget about any of those Marquis of Queensberry rules," Symington had advised the secretary of the army; now McCarthy demanded that the Missouri senator be disqualified from the investigation. The following evening, in Ripon, Wisconsin, he accused Symington of instigating the entire controversy in order to destroy Eisenhower and the Republican party.

The hearings themselves developed through a series of incidents, rather than by any logical exploration of the issues involved. There were typical McCarthy gambits—a cropped photograph of Schine and the secretary of the army, a phony letter from J. Edgar Hoover to Army Intelligence (G-2) "condensed" from a 15-page memorandum stolen from the files of the FBI or military intelligence. And there were violent personal attacks, for as McCarthy explained to one of the participants, he always followed a maxim taught him by "Indian Charlie," which was [as reported by the *New York Times*] "that if one was ever approached by another person in a not completely friendly fashion, one should start kicking at the other person as fast as possible below the belt until the other person was rendered helpless."

McCarthy Attacks Witnesses and His Peers

Some of McCarthy's attacks were aimed at people in no way involved in the hearings. On the very first day, for example, he demanded of General Miles Reber if he was aware that his brother [Samuel], the former deputy high commissioner of Germany, "was allowed to resign when charges that he was a bad security risk were made against him as a result of the investigations of this committee?" The charge was outrageously false, but it served McCarthy's purpose, temporarily diverting the hearings and casting a shadow on General Reber's testimony.

More often than not, however, McCarthy's attacks were directed at the other participants in the hearings. His office had prepared dossiers on each person, and in the fire of battle the senator would use these charges, whatever their nature, to bludgeon his opponents and throw them onto the defensive. He gathered some unspecified charges against Senator McClellan from enemies of the senator in Arkansas, but even McCarthy never quite dared to attack a senator so powerful and conservative. Nor did McCarthy himself attack Senator Jackson. After one especially acrimonious hearing, however, Roy Cohn marched over to minority counsel Robert F. Kennedy, and brandishing aloft a large folder marked "Jackson's record" he loudly threatened to "get Jackson."

Eisenhower was slowly but inevitably pulled into the conflict.

McCarthy's strongest blasts were directed against Stuart Symington. One of the charges in the Symington dossier stemmed from a teenage joyride Symington and two other boys had taken in a neighbor's car. The charge had been used against Symington during the 1952 campaign, and now McCarthy threatened to bring it up again. He would stride into the hearing room, throw his arm casually around Symington, and maliciously ask, "Stole any cars lately, Stu?" On June 9, before the cameras, McCarthy charged that the former secretary of the air force had "associated" with a Communist in a "study group" and that this was what lay behind his "smears" against the subcommittee and his attempts "to force an end to our investigation." This was also an accusation which McCarthy had first hurled at Symington in 1952 when he campaigned in Missouri on behalf of James P. Kem. The so-called study club referred to a series of meetings sponsored by Episcopalian Bishop Will Scarlett of Missouri. The Communist mentioned was William Sentner, the head of the United Electrical Workers of Missouri and the union representative with whom Symington had to deal as an executive for the Emerson Electric Manufacturing Company of St. Louis.

Then on one of the last days of the hearings McCarthy rose to another "point of order" and again accused Symington of trying to "smear" the subcommittee's staff and their work on the committee's files. The other senators were already gathering their papers and preparing to answer a roll call when Symington stood up, faced McCarthy, and angrily replied that "the files of what you call my staff, my director, my chief of staff, have been the sloppiest and most dangerously handled files that I have ever heard of since I have been in the Government." The caucus room burst into applause—not so much because of what Symington said but because of the sheer emotion with which he said it. The senators threaded their way through the crowd while McCarthy sputtered through his now familiar superlatives. "He runs away . . . the most dishonest . . . and most unfounded . . . upon some of the most outstanding young men . . . (whereupon, at 4:40 P.M. the hearing was recessed, to reconvene at 10 A.M. the following day, Tuesday, June 15, 1954)."

Welch Objects to the Smearing of Fisher

McCarthy's most celebrated attack was made on Frederick G. Fisher, a young member of army counsel Welch's law firm of Hale and Dorr in Boston. On the thirtieth day of the hearings, after a heated exchange between Welch and Roy Cohn, McCarthy interrupted with a "point of order" to charge that Fisher "has been for a number of years a member of an organization which was named, oh, years and years ago, as the legal bulwark of the Communist Party." When he finished, he was grinning at Welch across the table. Fisher had been originally chosen by Welch's assistant, James D. St. Clair, to help with the army defense and had accompanied Welch and St. Clair to Washington in early April. He had belonged, while a student at Harvard Law School, to the National Lawyers Guild, an organization now charged with Communist leanings. Although Fisher was an entirely respectable and very Republican member of Hale and Dorr, Welch had decided to send him back to

Boston lest there be any unpleasantness. The decision was hardly secret. McCarthy had even alluded to the incident in the formal countercharges he filed with the subcommittee on April 20. His lawyer, Edward Bennett Williams, and Roy Cohn had both prevailed upon him not to drag Fisher into the hearings, and the senator had promised them that he would not bring the matter up.

Once before the cameras, however, the senator seemed to slip all restraints. While Cohn pleadingly shook his head, McCarthy plunged into his attack on the young lawyer. Welch's reply was charged with emotion. "Until this moment I think I never really gauged your cruelty or your recklessness," he told McCarthy. He explained Fisher's background, his position in Hale and Dorr, and his brief membership in the Guild. Then he turned to McCarthy again: "Little did I dream you could be so reckless and so cruel as to do an injury to that lad. . . . If it were in my power to forgive you for your reckless cruelty, I [would] do so. I like to think I am a gentleman, but your forgiveness will have to come from some one other than me." McCarthy persisted, but Welch again cut him short. "Have you no sense of decency, sir, at long last? Have you left no sense of decency?" He arose and walked from the room, while the spectators broke into loud applause. As the subcommittee briefly recessed, McCarthy turned questioningly to those around him, turning his palms upward to ask "what did I do?"

Eisenhower Is Pulled into the Conflict

Throughout the course of the hearings President Eisenhower remained determined not to be drawn into the controversy. When he had to deal with McCarthy at all, he did so obliquely and through subordinates. Yet despite the president's determination, despite the best efforts of members of the Senate and the White House staff, Eisenhower was slowly but inevitably pulled into the conflict.

On May 14 army counsel John Adams refused to testify on the details of the January 21 meeting at which Sherman Adams had first directed him to prepare the army "chronology."[1] Three days later, on May 17, Eisenhower told Re-

1. John Adams, Sherman Adams, Herbert Brownell, Henry Cabot Lodge, and the majority members of the Permanent Subcommittee on Investigations met after McCarthy had threatened to subpoena the Loyalty and Security Appeals Board. On January 22, Republicans convinced McCarthy to not call the board.

publican congressional leaders that he would permit no testimony on private discussions within the Executive Department, and in a strong public letter to Secretary of Defense Wilson he directed that no such confidences be revealed, in order to preserve the integrity of the presidency, to maintain the proper separation of powers between the Executive and Congress, and to "preclude the exercise of arbitrary power by any branch of the Government."

McCarthy denounced the presidential order as an "iron curtain," and even the Democrats were reluctant to accede to this broad statement of executive privilege. McCarthy could not rest here, however, and on May 27 he declared that all federal employees should know that "it is their duty to give us any information which they have about graft, corruption, communism, treason, and that there is no loyalty to a superior officer which can tower above and beyond their loyalty to their country." His call was a plea for insubordination, a threat to the processes of orderly government, and a challenge to presidential prerogative which the administration could not ignore. The following day, in a statement approved by the president, Attorney General Brownell declared that the execution of laws was the sole and fundamental duty of the executive and "that responsibility can't be usurped by an individual who may seek to set himself above the laws of our land." For one brief instant the long-awaited confrontation between McCarthy and Eisenhower appeared to be at hand. The administration, however, crept back into its shell of protective silence, and the center stage was returned to the principals.

By May the Republicans were already working hard to bring the hearings to a close. On May 3 Senator Dirksen proposed that testimony be limited to McCarthy and Stevens, but immediately met strong opposition from the Democrats, who were determined to see the hearings continue until the administration faced up to McCarthy. The president, however, still had no intention of getting "into the gutter" with the senator. "I agree completely with your hope that the McCarthy-Army hearings be brought speedily and effectively to an end," he wrote a friend and supporter. "The Senate has sought means to bring this about; so far, unhappily, they have been unsuccessful."

On May 8 Dirksen again offered a plan for limiting the hearings, this time suggesting that the public phase of the investigation be closed after the Stevens and McCarthy testimony was taken and that any subsequent hearings proceed behind closed doors. McClellan and the Democrats resisted this maneuver, and after some initial wavering the army joined them in opposition to the motion. The proposal was defeated 4–3, with Chairman Mundt casting the tie-breaking vote.

On May 17, after John Adams had read President Eisenhower's letter to Secretary Wilson, Dirksen was ready with still another motion. This time he called for a one-week recess, ostensibly to study the procedural problems raised by Adams's refusal to testify about the January 21 conference with White House leaders. The motion read "recess," but the Republicans obviously hoped to use it to cool down the controversy, to take it behind closed doors, or perhaps to end it altogether. It passed on a straight party vote after Symington had denounced it as a "transparent device" to take McCarthy and Cohn off the hook.

The reaction to the maneuver was strong. McClellan reaffirmed the determination of the minority not to be diverted by side issues, and President Eisenhower now reversed himself in a news conference on May 19 and urged that the hearings be continued. Chairman Mundt scoffed at the idea that the recess was designed to end the hearings, and the following week the subcommittee resumed its work.

Senator Henry C. Dworshak presented yet another Republican motion on May 26, following a private conference by the majority members of the subcommittee. The Idaho Republican proposed that the charges against Assistant Secretary of Defense H. Struve Hensel and subcommittee staff director Francis Carr be dropped and that neither man be called to testify. The motion was important, not simply because it eliminated the two men as principals to the controversy, but because it also removed them as witnesses. Although Hensel's only part in the army-McCarthy controversy had been to sign a letter of transmittal forwarding the army "chronology" to Senator Potter, McCarthy had made him a main target for the formal countercharges he filed with the subcommittee on April 20. At an executive session on May 17, McCarthy admitted he had no evidence to show that Hensel had been involved in the controversy, but he refused to withdraw the charges because, as he told Hensel, he would look like "a damn fool."

The case of Frank Carr was quite different, for although the army testimony showed that he had been a rather passive accomplice to Cohn's improprieties, he remained one of the most important witnesses to the various activities of McCarthy, Cohn, and others. Welch pleaded with Dworshak to split his motion in two, and he begged the majority not to pass it, but to no avail. The motion carried on a straight party vote.

By June 8 both the army and McCarthy had given up any hope of a clear-cut decision and were moving toward an agreement with the subcommittee majority on ending the hearings. Once again Dirksen took the initiative, proposing that the hearings be ended in one week. Private Schine, the amazing young man who had done so much to precipitate the hearings, was not to be called at all. The Democrats were just as determined to keep the investigation open. "I am not going to be a party to eliminating the subject of the controversy," declared Senator Jackson. Once again, however, the motion carried on a party vote, and the hearings at long last wound toward an end. . . .

The Republicans Shun McCarthy

The political stress created by the hearings was felt most acutely by the moderate Republicans who had long tried to avoid or ignore the McCarthy problem altogether. From across the entire country, storm warnings from Republican leaders poured into the White House. "There is a growing impatience with the Republican Party," declared Congressman George H. Bender, the Republican candidate for the Senate in Ohio. "McCarthyism has become a synonym for witch-hunting, star-chamber methods and the denial of those civil liberties which have distinguished our country in its historic growth." If we don't do something about McCarthy, warned a New Hampshire national committeeman, "we are going to lose a lot of votes." In Nebraska a Republican leader reported that everyone on the State Central Committee had agreed "that our candidates are being harmed by this public spectacle." "If we are to win the November election, we shall need the support of the Independents, many Democrats and the 'liberal' Republicans," complained an Iowa Republican leader to Sherman Adams. "It is now time for the Republican Party to repudiate Joe McCarthy before he drags them all to defeat," declared Palmer

Hoyt of the *Denver Post*. From California to New York, from Tennessee to Vermont, Republican leaders expressed worry, anger, and frustration over the disruption McCarthy had caused. "If the facts could be proven," grumbled one Texas banker, "I am sure he is in the employ of the New Dealers."

In the Senate, Republicans felt the same pressures. "I cannot begin to tell you how many people I have heard around these parts expressing their intention to vote for a Democratic senator as a means of supplying the necessary votes to eliminate the junior Senator from Wisconsin," wrote a New Jersey Republican to Senator Robert C. Hendrickson. "If my mail reflects any degree of accuracy, we are in for trouble as a result of the hearings," agreed Hendrickson. "I wonder if you gentlemen there in Washington fully realize what this is doing to the Republican party," complained a Nebraska Republican to Senator Hugh Butler. "I will guess with you that hereabouts it is making more Democratic votes than helping the Republican party," added a local banker. "My own personal views coincide with the general run of Republicans who are engaged in fund raising," wrote the chairman of the Republican National Finance Committee to Karl Mundt. "The opinion of a large majority . . . is that the McCarthy-Stevens hearings are a disgraceful affair and the sooner they finish the better for the party."

But all this did not change the underlying balance of power. McCarthy still had the unyielding support of eight to ten Senate bitter-enders and through them considerable leverage over the Republican leadership in Congress and the White House. McCarthy had remained in power through the acquiescence of the Senate body, not its active support. The army-McCarthy hearings had increased the instability of the "McCarthy balance," but they had not destroyed it altogether. McCarthy had recovered on countless other occasions and even now, as the hearings closed, he was already talking of new and expanded investigations of the army, the CIA, and the defense industry.

But none of the senator's proposed investigations ever materialized. Before the army-McCarthy hearings ended, Senator Ralph Flanders arose in the Senate to initiate a resolution which would ultimately lead to McCarthy's condemnation. The Flanders resolution was a dramatic and probably decisive attempt to end the McCarthy interregnum and to reclaim the honor and dignity of the Senate.

4

McCarthy's Role in the Red Scare Has Been Exaggerated

M.J. Heale

M.J. Heale is a McCarthy scholar who is the recipient of a fellowship from the American Council of Learned Societies and grants from the British Academy, the American Philosophical Society, and Lancaster University. In this selection, Heale describes how red scare politics were used well before McCarthy. He is critical of the term *McCarthyism*, which refers to a period that preceded the senator and continued after his censure and death. According to Heale, red scare politics were the result of complex social processes and certain key events that made the United States ripe for such a phenomenon. To be fully understood, red scare politics should be examined at the state level and not confined to the study of one individual.

S ome years ago a conference held at Harvard University on the topic 'Anticommunism and the US' was advertised by a poster presenting the brooding, baleful face of Senator Joe McCarthy. The image was a powerful one but it was also misleading, because, as most of the conference participants knew perfectly well, the late Senator had done little or nothing to create the phenomenon he had come to personify. McCarthy is not synonymous with McCarthyism, even less with American anticommunism, and his troubled presence has sometimes obscured those historical processes that helped to make his career possible. Over the

Excerpted from *McCarthy's Americans: Red Scare Politics in State and Nation, 1935–1965*, by M.J. Heale (Athens: The University of Georgia Press, 1998). Copyright © 1998 by M.J. Heale. Reprinted with permission.

last generation several scholars have sought to reach beyond the image, and a number of superb studies now illuminate parts of what might be called McCarthy's hinterland, but the process remains incomplete. Probably no area has been as patchily addressed as that represented by the basic building blocks of the American system of government, the American states themselves. . . .

Red Scare Politics Began Before McCarthy

One limitation of the term McCarthyism is that it slights the long history of red scare politics in the United States before Joe McCarthy's high-pitched whine was first heard in the United States Senate. Domestic anticommunism, that tendency to espy a red enemy within, has been a primary feature of American politics since the late nineteenth century. At times the fear of subversion, or at least the exploitation of that fear, has been so intense and pervasive as to constitute a red scare, as in the Haymarket Affair of 1886–87, the Palmer Raids of 1919–20, and the McCarthyism of the early 1950s. This is not the place to explore the political and cultural roots of American anticommunism, but any study of a particular episode needs to be aware of that resilient tradition. More than most societies, Americans have been defined by shared values rather than by ancient institutions, and have thus always been sensitive to the prospect of ideological subversion. The peculiar burden placed on political ideology in the United States has been the greater because of the variegated nature of its people. A diverse society has not easily cohered, and conceptions of Americanism have been pressed into service in attempts to strengthen the social fabric. But patriotism can take different forms, and may divide as well as unite. Both the American Civil Liberties Union and the John Birch Society have grounded their legitimacy in American conceptions of freedom. [McCarthyites] may seem capable of the most egregiously partisan and cynical behaviour, but they were also conditioned by values which stretched back to the beginnings of the American republic. Red scares have been part of the American political process, inseparable from its instrumentality and its ideology, not aberrations or the products of mindless hysteria or the spawn of gifted demagogues.

But even the red scare associated with Senator McCarthy was not triggered by his celebrated speech at

Wheeling, West Virginia, in February 1950. Several scholars have pointed to the significance of episodes and policies
associated with President Harry Truman's first beleaguered
term, and some have emphasized the rightward thrusts of
American politics during the later part of the New Deal, as
illustrated by the foundation of the House Committee on
Un-American Activities (HUAC) in 1938. . . . A focus on
state politics emphasizes the value of this longer perspective. One way of perceiving the Senator's excesses is as part
of a political cycle which first emerged in the mid-1930s and
took two decades or more to run its course. In several states,
the political configurations which were to make possible the
red scare politics of the Cold War years had first taken
shape in the 1930s, if not earlier. McCarthyism was not so
much an aberration as a product of long-term processes that
favoured conservative politics. In some states, indeed, Mc-
Carthyite political formations survived after a fashion and
were provoked to new spasms by the radicalism of the
1960s. The revitalized conservatism of Richard Nixon and
Ronald Reagan was not created in a vacuum and owed
something to tensions which Senator McCarthy and the little McCarthys in the states had exploited. They had helped
to expose the fragility of what is sometimes known as the
New Deal political order.

If McCarthyism was in part made possible by an older
rightward trend in American politics, key events of the 1940s
and 1950s undoubtedly furthered the cause. Scholars have
rightly pointed to the demoralizing impact of the course of
foreign affairs on both public opinion and policy-makers,
most evidenced by the extension of Soviet control over eastern Europe after the Second World War and by the unnerv-
ing 'loss' of China and the revelation of Soviet possession of
the A-bomb in 1949. The responses of the Truman administration and of the public at large to the escalating threat of
world communism helped Senator McCarthy and his
brethren to move from the political wings to centre stage.
Yet a state-level examination raises questions both about the
critical junctures in international relations and about the
Senator's influence. For one thing, anticommunist politics
did not emerge simultaneously throughout the land. In some
states red scares arrived early and in others late, suggesting
that external stimuli of themselves have limited explanatory
power, that as much attention needs to be paid to internal

political pressures. But if there was a foreign crisis which had a clear impact on state politics it was the outbreak of the Korean War. Because McCarthy's heyday was almost coincident with the Korean War, it is difficult to disentangle the influence of the two on the extensive political terrain outside Washington, but the evidence suggests that Korea was more important than McCarthy (or even other foreign policy reverses) in precipitating anticommunist programmes.

It may be that both national and state governments exaggerated the prospect of a Third World War in these years. But anxiety over Korea cannot simply be dismissed as irrational. Recently some scholars, while contemptuous of the irresponsible antics of Senator McCarthy, have presented moderate anticommunism on the foreign and domestic fronts as a reasonable response to a real and present danger. They have identified a threat not only in the murderous Soviet regime but also inside the United States, where there was both an active Communist party which sympathized with the Soviet Union and authentic Soviet espionage. This view implies a correlation between Communist and anticommunist activity, and whether one existed is a question that can be asked of state politics. . . . But the evidence also suggests that the rationality of anticommunist behaviour often reflected more a self-regarding partisanship than a selfless patriotism. The threat of domestic communism was invariably magnified by the operations and culture of American politics.

The Red Scare in the State Arena

A study of state politics also makes possible a consideration of other important questions scholars have raised about McCarthyism. It has been held that McCarthyism was primarily the product of populist or grassroots pressures revolting against a political establishment, that is a form of mass insurgency fuelled by status anxieties or resentments. More recently responsibility has instead been substantially assigned to various elites, whether presidential administrations or powerful institutions like the FBI. The political establishment in Washington or the major parties engaged in conventional partisan politics, in this view, far from being the targets of grassroots anger, were the prime creators of this Frankenstein's Monster. Yet, with some valuable exceptions, neither perspective has been much informed by research at state or local level. If it is necessary to establish whether McCarthyism was a populist phenomenon, welling upwards through the American political system, or an elitist phenomenon, introduced at the top and trickling downwards, it seems logical to examine the states, for they were the arenas in which local and national pressures met. . . .

But a study of the states should reveal more than the direction of McCarthyite pressures. The state arena provides a context in which at least some of the ingredients of red scare politics might be identified and their interaction examined. Quite apart from the inseparability of national and state politics, it was also the case that the state McCarthyites often blazed the trails for their federal counterparts. Controlling sedition and subversion, after all, had traditionally been a state responsibility, and by the time the federal government formally moved into this sphere with the Smith Act of 1940, the state statute books bristled with laws directed at anarchists and Communists. . . . Congressmen fought the red menace with HUAC, but several states had their own little HUACs, some of which anticipated the techniques used by the various congressional inquisitors of the 1950s. Loyalty oaths were widely deployed by the states before President Truman introduced his loyalty programme for federal employees in 1947; the Communist party was even outlawed by one state some years before Congress contrived to do something similar with the Communist Control Act of 1954. This is not to suggest that the federal measures and probes of the 1940s and 1950s owed their force to state example. Sometimes the states took the initiative and sometimes the federal government did, and the latter could generally exert more influence. The dynamics of party politics, the Cold War and the national security state did exert powerful pressures from the centre, but they also need to be seen as operating in a constitutional structure which allowed the states significant autonomy. Indeed, this author has argued elsewhere that it was the very flimsiness of the federal government which in part explains the historic strength of anticommunism in the United States. . . .

The Result of a Complex Social Process

Some limitations of the term McCarthyism have already been indicated; it sits poorly with a story which began before the Second World War and continued after the Wisconsin senator's death. Further, in some accounts the term has been used to direct attention to the political purge of the Cold War era and its victims. That is a vital issue which other scholars have addressed, and it is not the intention here to document every judicial proceeding or job loss. The term red scare politics is meant to suggest a somewhat different concern, one which allows a focus on the operations of state politics, which may witness the redbaiting of party opponents as well as the hounding of suspect employees. . . .

McCarthyism—or red scare politics—was a complex phenomenon, and can be explained only by addressing the American political structure as a whole and by reference to a variety of pressures. While the political passions which peaked in the 1950s had their roots in the 1930s, it makes no sense to try to understand them without considerable attention to the Cold War and the imperatives of the national security state. Without these later pressures the anticommunist persuasion, strong though it already was, would not have achieved the potency it did. But there were other essential ingredients too, among them what in another context has been called reactionary populism. Historians have lately been recognizing that the conservative rejection of the celebrated consensualism of the 1950s was not confined to the unreconstructed rich, and that distaste for New Deal liberalism or the liberal consensus extended to many workers (and to some of the middle and professional classes too). A form of reactionary politics also flourished in the South, and again Senator McCarthy and his ilk would not have enjoyed the prominence they did without the critical role played by this section in the American political system. Yet complex phenomenon though McCarthyism was, ultimately the red scare politics of the 1940s and 1950s were an expression of a kind of political fundamentalism, or rather of a variety of fundamentalisms. The focus of some early scholars on the fears of those of modest status may have been somewhat misleading, for anxieties were liberally distributed throughout society. The term status anxiety may be inappropriate, but at many levels there were people and interests clinging fiercely to traditional forms. In different and subtle ways, the precepts of class, race and religion were militating against the emergence of a genuinely multicultural society. For many Americans, McCarthyism was a cry of pain for the sundry worlds they had lost.

5

McCarthyism, Self-Censorship, and the Loss of Civil Liberties

Ellen Schrecker

Ellen Schrecker is an expert on McCarthyism who has written and edited several books on the subject. In this excerpt from her book *Many Are the Crimes*, Schrecker describes the adverse impact of McCarthyism on the civil rights movement and the publishing, film, and television industries. Although resistance to racial equality was already very strong in certain regions, according to Schrecker, anticommunism became a tool of the dominant group to oppress minorities and prevent advances by the civil rights movement. Also, the mentality of McCarthyism generated an atmosphere of fear and repression conducive to self-censorship within various creative and intellectual circles. While the government may not have overtly oppressed the populace with mandatory censoring of materials from these sectors, the industries themselves regulated the flow of ideas, sometimes by peremptorily censoring their own products.

[M]cCarthyism caused a] rollback within the civil rights movement, though it is important not to overestimate its impact. Racism was formidable enough in itself. And all of the initiatives that McCarthyism aborted might well have foundered anyhow when confronted by the strong currents of racism in American society. Nonetheless, a case can be made that the anticommunist crusade, besides isolating an important group of activists, deflected the civil rights movement from pressing for economic, as well as legal and political, change. Communists were, of course, deeply involved in the struggle for black equality. The CP [Communist Party], one of its main Southern leaders noted, "really meant business on racism." From [labor union] Mine-Mill's registration of black voters in Birmingham, Alabama, to the picket lines that local chapters of the Congress of American Women threw up outside segregated swimming pools in the North, the communist movement battled segregation as indefatigably as any civil rights group. For many black Communists, in fact, the party *was* a civil rights group. Marginalizing it and its white and black adherents, thus, changed the struggle against racial discrimination.

The Effect of McCarthyism on the Civil Rights Movement

Within the South, McCarthyism eliminated options and narrowed the struggle for black equality. Again, it is a question of lost opportunities. For a brief moment in the late forties, there was the possibility that the region's organized black workers and its more liberal whites might have been able to build an interracial civil rights movement with a strong grassroots base in the African American community. Had such a movement existed in the mid-1950s, it might have provided a counterweight to the hardcore segregationists who mobilized against the *Brown* decision. It might, in other words, have influenced the Southern moderates to implement integration rather than resist it. But the anticommunist crusade anathematized the individuals and destroyed the institutions that would have provided both the leadership and the community support for mobilizing a vigorous mass movement. Without that movement, most civil rights groups in the 1950s were conservative, respectable, and small—and posed little challenge to the entrenched Southern way of life.

The left-wing unions were at the heart of the stillborn movement. Many of them had been functioning as quasi–civil rights groups for years. The communist-led Food, Tobacco, and Agricultural Workers Union (FTA) Local 22 in Winston-Salem, North Carolina, exemplified this type of rights-based unionism. The local represented the thousands of primarily black and female workers who held menial jobs in the R.J. Reynolds Company's huge tobacco plant. Like other left-led unions, Local 22 not only gave its members the usual economic benefits of unionization, but also offered them a vibrant social life with a wide array of classes, clubs, and cultural events. In addition, it gave them a new sense of self-worth, enabling them to challenge the demeaning way in which the company had traditionally treated its powerless black women workers. Because the union recognized the interconnection between its own struggles and those of the larger community, it encouraged its members to vote and join the NAACP—efforts that helped elect an African American to Winston-Salem's board of aldermen and obtain better services for the city's black residents.

But Local 22 could not withstand the anticommunist crusade. R.J. Reynolds had never wanted the union. In 1947, the company's refusal to accede to the demand for a wage hike provoked a bitter strike that attracted HUAC's [House Un-American Activities Committee] attention. The hearings highlighted the communist connections of Local 22's leaders and weakened its support within the broader community. Encouraged by the CIO [Congress of Industrial Organizations], rival unions took advantage of the FTA's failure to sign the Taft-Hartley affidavits and raided the local. The company damaged the union further by redesigning its manufacturing process to eliminate the jobs of the local's most loyal black members. By the time the CIO expelled the FTA in 1950, Local 22 was no longer functioning. Winston-Salem's civil rights movement foundered as well. The NAACP chapter that had swelled from 11 to 1,991 members between 1942 and 1946 fell below 500 during the 1950s and lost its working-class orientation. Middle-class blacks regained their leadership of the civil rights movement and tried to accommodate themselves to the white power structure.

Similar struggles, with similar outcomes, occurred in Birmingham, Memphis, New Orleans, and elsewhere. The destruction of the progressive unions in the South stilled the voices that sought economic change along with racial equality. The civil rights groups that operated during the 1950s concentrated only on legal and political issues; the South's increasingly beleaguered unions did not challenge Jim Crow.

Middle-class whites who might have worked for integration in the South were also silenced during the Mc-

Carthy years. Though some of these people were in or near the party and others were in the left-wing unions, many were New Deal liberals like Clifford and Virginia Durr, who just wanted to democratize their native region. They and the organizations they worked with, like the Southern Conference for Human Welfare or the Highlander Folk School, encountered serious red-baiting. Highlander, which trained union activists and civil rights workers, managed to survive the onslaught. The SCHW, an interracial body that tried to stimulate support for liberal reforms, did not. Internal conflicts and a 1947 HUAC report listing the subversive connections of its leaders did the group in. By the end of the 1940s, only a tiny band of white Southerners, most of them in the SCHW's beleaguered successor, the Southern Conference Educational Fund [SCEF], would dare to call for integration.

Within the South, McCarthyism eliminated options and narrowed the struggle for black equality.

Anticommunism proved invaluable to white supremacists during the 1940s and 1950s. It provided them with a more up-to-date and respectable cover than mere racism and hooked them into a national network of right-wing activists. At the same time it reinforced their traditional contention that outside agitators were behind the move for civil rights. "The attempt to abolish segregation in the South," the Alabama Citizens Councils explained, "is fostered and directed by the Communist party." That allegation increased the South's traditional penalties for whites who opposed Jim Crow. Not only would these people face the social isolation and economic sanctions that racial dissidents ordinarily incurred, they would also have to contend with McCarthyism. . . .

As the civil rights movement began to revive in the mid-1950s, Southern politicians responded by adopting the machinery of anticommunism. Almost every state had its own little HUAC clone or registration statute modeled on the 1950 McCarran Act. Several states even outlawed the NAACP. Long after they had lost their mainstream audiences in the North, professional witnesses like J.B. Matthews and Manning Johnson traveled around Dixie peddling their tales of communist infiltration and incitement. Instead of harassing Communists, however, Southern investigators usually took on civil rights activists. Florida's Legislative Investigating Committee, which also pursued gays and lesbians, launched contempt charges against the president of Miami's NAACP for refusing to turn over its membership lists; Louisiana's Un-American Activities Committee raided the headquarters of SCEF and indicted three of its officers for sedition. There were economic sanctions as well; membership in the NAACP or support for integration was as bad for the career of a state employee or college teacher in the South as taking the Fifth Amendment before HUAC was in the North.

But none of the Florida or Louisiana defendants went to prison. The Supreme Court, though still upholding the convictions of alleged Communists like Carl Braden, did not countenance the political repression of civil rights workers. Its position reveals the ironic fact that anticommunism actually bolstered the struggle for racial equality. The Cold War encouraged the liberal establishment to embrace integration. When the Truman administration formally committed itself to civil rights, it was not only responding to the increased political clout of blacks in the North and the need to win liberals away from Henry Wallace in 1948, but also to the recognition that, as Secretary of State Dean Acheson noted, "The existence of discrimination against minority groups in this country has an adverse effect on our relations with other countries." The United States, in other words, might not be able to win the Cold War until it cleaned up its own act. As long as the civil rights movement was itself suitably anticommunist, the nation's political establishment gave it considerable support. An implicit deal had been made: liberals would sacrifice reds for blacks.

The deal unraveled a bit in the early 1960s, when it became clear that the leaders of the new mass-based movements, like Martin Luther King and the young radicals in the Student Nonviolent Coordinating Committee, did not share the anticommunist instincts of the Cold War liberals. SNCC imposed no political tests and was willing to work with the likes of SCEF, the Bradens, and the National Lawyers Guild, much to the despair of the liberal establishment, which sought unsuccessfully to make the group sever its ties with the NLG attorneys who were helping it in Mississippi.

King, however, capitulated. Two of his top aides had once been in the party; and [J. Edgar] Hoover, who believed that the civil rights movement was communist-inspired, passed that information to the president, who in turn forced the civil rights leader to break with the men. King's house-cleaning did not end the pressure on him, though it shifted from standard red-baiting to a much nastier form of black-mail. The bugs and wiretaps that the FBI had planted to get evidence about the subversive activities of King's entourage discovered the sexual ones instead. Since Hoover was con-vinced that the SCLC leader was a communist pawn, he had no compunctions about using that information as the basis of a vicious COINTELPRO campaign against King.

To the extent that the smear campaign cut into the SCLC leader's effectiveness—and it certainly did—it dam-aged the civil rights movement as well. By the mid-sixties, that movement had begun to unravel. Obviously, anticom-munism was only one, and hardly the most important, ele-ment in that tragic disintegration. The Vietnam War, the movement's own internal conflicts, and the deep-seated racism within American society all played a larger role. Still, McCarthyism did have an impact. From the start, it had narrowed the movement's agenda, separated it from poten-tial allies, and kept it from seriously challenging the poverty that blighted the lives of most African Americans. Even when someone like Martin Luther King, Jr., called for eco-nomic as well as racial equality, the McCarthy era had so thoroughly erased class issues from the political agenda that his words did not get heard.

The Effect on the Cultural Arena

Doors closed in the cultural arena as well. Again, it is a mat-ter of imponderables and missed opportunities. Nonetheless, it is clear that the anticommunist crusade transformed the mental contours of American life, changing the way that mil-lions of ordinary people thought about themselves and their society. Gone was the Popular Front mind-set with its glori-fication of the little man and its celebration of labor and cul-tural diversity. Gone, too, was the class consciousness and the emphasis on collective struggle that had pervaded so much of American culture during the 1930s and 1940s.

Even the language through which that view of the world

was articulated disappeared. Scholars were particularly sensitive to the transformation. "You'd talk about 'industrialization' instead of 'industrial capitalism,'" an MIT Americanist recalled. Class-laden terminology that was common in the mainstream media during the 1940s was gone by the 1950s. References to "working stiffs" disappeared and the word "boss" lost its pejorative connotations. By 1963, a leading Protestant bishop threatened to quit the March on Washington if the Student Nonviolent Coordinating Committee's chair, John Lewis, used the words "masses" and "revolution" in his speech. A recent study of the topics cited in the *Readers' Guide to Periodical Literature* notes a similar linguistic shift.

At the same time, American culture mellowed, changing its tone as well as its tune. In thousands of subtle ways, the men and women who produced that culture—teachers, writers, artists, and movie directors among others—eliminated its sharp edges. When a group of sociologists interviewed nearly 2,500 academics in 1955, they found that hundreds of them had consciously modulated their voices. Not only had they suppressed their political opinions, but, like the professor who revised an article to read "TV is 97 per cent tinsel" instead of "97 per cent trash," they tried to seem less confrontational. From Harvard to Hollywood, moderation had become the passion of the day.

Self-Censorship in the Publishing Industry

McCarthyism bore much of the responsibility for that banality. Though self-censorship was common, it rested on a base of overt repression. Even in the publishing industry, where, if anywhere, free expression should have been protected, many were the authors who consigned controversial manuscripts to their desk drawers because they had been told their work could not be published. The evidence here is anecdotal but indicates a fairly widespread pattern of suppression. Communist writers, of course, were completely unacceptable. Marketability was not, as it presumably is today, at issue. In 1951, after serving a prison term for contempt, the bestselling novelist Howard Fast had to publish *Spartacus* on his own. Though it became a movie and sold hundreds of thousands of copies, the FBI had made sure that no major publisher would touch the book. Fast was not the only blacklisted novelist. A former editor at Harper's recalls seeing an enthusiastic reader's report from the mid-fifties that complained about being unable to publish Doris Lessing's second novel. It was wonderful, but the writer was a Communist.

Sometimes the subject matter, not the author, got censored. After all, as writer Tillie Olsen noted, the fifties was a "time when you didn't have books about people who had to work for a living." Nor were there many mainstream trade books published about the witch-hunt. Clifford Durr was in the midst of negotiating the size of his advance for a book about the loyalty program when the Korean War broke out and the publisher backed down. The book, it seemed, was no longer "saleable." Similar market concerns kept other publishers from taking on the casebook about civil liberties that Yale Law School professor Thomas Emerson wrote in the early 1950s. A small house published the book—and did quite well by it. Other writers faced similar difficulties when they wrote about unpopular subjects or individuals. Harper's turned down Eleanor Flexner's classic history of the women's movement because it devoted too much attention to blacks. And before he could publish his *Famous Negro Music Makers*, Langston Hughes had to excise all mention of Paul Robeson; otherwise, he was told, the book would be barred from school libraries. Other writers got the message. They stopped writing about unacceptable topics, turned to genres like science fiction, or else stopped writing. And, significantly, they stopped founding small literary magazines.

Nonetheless, politically incorrect literature didn't completely disappear during the McCarthy era; there were always marginal presses and even desk drawers. Writers could still write, even if they could not reach a large audience. People in other media faced more crippling barriers. Paul Robeson, for example, simply disappeared from public view. Probably no other individual was as heavily censored. By the time he became the first person barred from American television early in 1950, the most charismatic black actor and singer of his generation had already become a nonperson. In 1949, four years after the NAACP had awarded him its prestigious Spingarn medal, it left his name off its list of past winners. By the mid-fifties, hundreds of other men and women in the entertainment industry were experiencing the same treatment. They, too, had been forced out of show business and denied access to an audience. That exclusion profoundly affected the nation's mass media, though it is sometimes hard to separate out the specific effects of the blacklist from the overall conservative backlash of the early Cold War.

The Effect on Motion Pictures and TV

Certainly, at the time, observers believed McCarthyism had influenced the content of motion pictures and TV. Such, after all, had been the goal of HUAC, the FBI, and the film industry's right-wingers. They were determined to stamp out the subversive messages that they believed were creeping onto the nation's movie screens: and to a large extent they succeeded. The anticommunist crusade and the blacklist that it imposed ended Hollywood's brief flirtation with the real world and ensured that the fledgling television industry would never even begin one.

In that aborted social democratic moment right after the end of World War II, when a revitalized labor-left liberal coalition might have emerged, the major studios were making films about social problems. Though it is hard today to realize that the 1948 movie *The Boy with Green Hair* was intended to counter racial prejudice, the film and the others of its genre did indicate a new sensibility and raise the possibility of a more engaged and socially conscious American cinema. Antisemitism, alcoholism, lynching, mental illness, even miscegenation, appeared on screen, though often in an oblique manner that perpetrated traditional racial and ethnic stereotypes. Still, real issues were raised. The Academy Award–winning *The Best Years of Our Lives*, for example, not only dealt with unemployment, insensitive bankers, and physical disabilities, but also showed a few black faces in crowd scenes. Communists and their allies were disproportionately involved in making these movies, but the impetus for them came, as it always did within the film industry, from the top. The 1947 HUAC hearings brought this experiment to a halt; "social problem" films decreased from 20.9 percent of the studios' output in 1947 to 9 percent in 1950 and 1951.

Part of the retrenchment was economic. These serious films did not make money. And, during the early Cold War years, the anticommunist crusade was only one of Hollywood's many problems. Not only was it losing its audience to television and suburban life, but it also had to restructure its distribution system after losing a major lawsuit. The film world responded to the crisis by instituting the blacklist and dumbing down. It did not want to put anything on the screen that might offend any segment of its shrinking audience. Musicals, westerns, war films, and technologically innovative blockbusters filled the nation's movie theaters. There was, however, an exception; during the height of the blacklist, about fifty unprofitable but explicitly anticommunist films were made.

McCarthyism did, thus, reach the screen, though the hardcore propaganda of *The Red Menace* or *I Was a Communist for the FBI* won no acclaim. The most effective cinematic artifact of the witch-hunt was *On the Waterfront*, Elia Kazan's 1954 depiction of a longshoreman who testifies against the gangsters in control of his union. Though the film's working-class milieu reflected a Popular Front grittiness, its message was profoundly conservative. Not only did it glorify the role of the informer and thus presumably justify Kazan and his colleagues' own recent collaboration with HUAC, but it also hurt the labor movement by portraying union leaders in a negative way.

It is clear that the anticommunist crusade transformed the mental contours of American life, changing the way that millions of ordinary people thought about themselves and their society.

Equally conservative, though less obviously political, were the messages that the ordinary genre films of the period purveyed: the good guy/bad guy polarization of the Westerns, the unthinking patriotism of the war movies, the global triumphalism of the Bible epics, and the constricted sexuality of the romantic comedies. Hollywood was selling an escapist oeuvre that indirectly sanctioned the ostensibly homogenized society of Cold War America by keeping blacks, workers, and uppity women off the screen. Never brave to begin with, the film industry's panicky response to the anticommunist crusade had simply intensified its traditional reluctance to challenge conventional mores or question the status quo.

Timid as Hollywood was, the infant television industry was even more so. It was, after all, just beginning to reach a mass audience when McCarthyism hit. As a result, both its structure and its content were profoundly shaped by the blacklist era. The pressures on the industry to behave itself and shed its politically tainted workers were enormous. J. Edgar Hoover forced the FCC [Federal Communications Commission] to deny licenses to applicants who "have affiliated themselves sympathetically with the activities of the communist movement." The main pressure came from the private sector. The sponsors and their advertising agencies, who in the 1940s and 1950s actually exercised direct control over programs, were terrified of controversy. As producer Mark Goodson noted, the agencies above all wanted to keep out of trouble. "The favorite slogan along Madison Avenue is 'Why buy yourself a headache?'" They thus forced the networks to capitulate to the professional anti-Communists and drop hundreds, perhaps thousands, of actors, writers, and technicians from their payrolls.

A lot of talent was lost. Between April 1955 and March 1956, producer David Susskind could not get clearance for a third of the five thousand names that he submitted for one of his programs. The men and women who did get through were hardly controversial. But, as one CBS executive complained, "The trouble with people who've never joined anything and therefore are 'safe' for us to use is that they usually aren't very good writers or actors or producers or, hell, human beings."

The blacklist was not, of course, entirely responsible for what Susskind deplored as the "steady deterioration" of the industry's offerings. Sponsors censored content as well as personnel, eliminating anything that aroused controversy or detracted from the consumerist message they were trying to convey. Naturally, programs about racial issues or civil liberties were verboten, but so, too, were ones that showed businessmen as villains or featured ordinary people with real-life problems. By the early fifties, the television industry had become so timid that, as one critic noted at the time, "virtually everything from pregnancy to freedom of religion is considered a controversial subject, leaving almost nothing except homicide as a fit topic to enter our houses."

Most of the entertainment that reached the nation's living rooms during the 1950s supported the status quo. Quiz shows celebrated capital accumulation. Westerns and crime stories offered simplistic morality tales that got resolved by violence. Sitcoms reinforced traditional gender roles. And what passed for documentaries were often [recycled] World War II propaganda films produced by the armed forces. The news was equally oversimplified and militaristic. Except when they handled special events like the Army-McCarthy hearings, networks rarely had the resources to cover stories live. They usually relied on government briefings and official footage, especially when dealing with warfare and foreign policy. Public affairs programming was predictably bland. The networks consciously decided not to run editorials in order to avoid controversy. Though television inherited talk-show panels from radio, it narrowed the range of opinions expressed on them. Moreover, the conviviality that suffused these programs trivialized the issues they dealt with and reinforced the notion that Americans had nothing to disagree about.

Not much has changed. Though the mass media did open up slightly during the 1960s, the patterns of institutional restraint and self-censorship established during the McCarthy era are still around. So, too, are the limitations on the range of issues that receive exposure.

6

McCarthyism Created a Liberal Political Backlash

Arthur Herman

Arthur Herman, a professor of history at George Mason University, analyzes the political landscape in the wake of the McCarthy era. Fear of communism and red scare politics were at a high pitch during that period, which the Wisconsin senator exploited as a political tool to forward his own interests. According to Herman, McCarthy's reckless style actually benefited the liberals of the Democratic Party, helping to pave the way for the election of John F. Kennedy to the presidency. Although some of McCarthy's concerns may have been valid, his zeal and paranoid style contributed to an anti-anticommunist backlash that led to more liberal foreign and domestic policies. In Herman's view, McCarthy inadvertently forwarded the Communist cause as a result of his careless crusade against it.

During the censure debate, *Time* magazine had hinted that McCarthy's fall might actually *help* the continuing investigation of Communist subversion. It was a fatuous hope. Interest in investigations in both the House and the Senate plummeted. When the Internal Security committee held its public hearings in the mid-fifties, only two newspapers still regularly sent reporters. Antisubversion lost whatever headline appeal it had ever had, and those who had suffered under its strictures now wanted revenge.

With McCarthy gone, anti-Stalinist liberals found themselves at war again with the old Popular Front mentality, which the cold war had driven from the scene. A host of intellectuals and writers and ex–fellow travelers had chafed under the restrictions about appearing pro-Soviet or too anti-American. . . .

A Victory for Anti-Anti-Communists

McCarthy's disgrace allowed the anti-anti-Communists to retake the high moral ground they had lost since the Nazi-Soviet Pact and the [Alger] Hiss [spy] case. The anti-anti-Communist left got its next chance with Harvey Matusow. Matusow had been an FBI informant on Communist Party activities in New York, testifying at trials of CPUSA [Communist Party] officials and making a small name for himself as a lecturer and author. His 1951 article on Communist infiltration in the military, "Reds in Khaki," may have helped to steer McCarthy's attention toward the Army. Matusow even worked with him for a time. But then law enforcement officials began to get leery about Matusow's increasingly sensational claims and his emotional instability, and he lost his audience. So Matusow skipped to the other side. With the help of publisher and secret Communist Albert Kahn, he released a startling self-exposé called *False Witness*, which detailed how he had lied about the Communist threat and charged that others were doing the same. Its title was a play on the most famous anti-Communist memoir of all, Whittaker Chambers' *Witness*, with the clear implication that ex-Communists who are anti-Communists are *all* liars. The publisher, and reviewers on the progressive left, touted the book in triumph. Exposure of the "cropped photo" and the "purloined FBI letter" during the Army-McCarthy hearings had suggested that the antisubversive cause relied on false evidence, and now [Communist-turned-FBI-informant Harvey] Matusow (who had testified from time to time before McCarthy's committee) confirmed it. Red hunting really was just a phony excuse to attack New Deal liberalism—as the popular slogan had it, Republicans spell "FDR" H-I-S-S.

McCarthy's disgrace had completely vindicated men like [Dean] Acheson, [George] Marshall, and [Philip] Jessup in the eyes of the media and opinion makers. Now that vindication rippled out to include hosts of others—not just Owen Lattimore or the China hands or other "innocent victims" of McCarthy's attacks, but those whose guilt had seemed more certain, such as Alger Hiss. If Hiss's disgrace had given McCarthy credibility in 1950, now the dynamic was reversed. *The Nation*, the old standard-bearer of the Popular Front, and its fellow-traveling editor, Carey McWilliams, carried on a decade-long campaign to prove that Hiss had been framed. His assistant Fred J. Cook would later publish a deeply negative and influential account of the McCarthy years, *The Nightmare Decade*. Hiss was released from prison and made his first public appearance in April 1956 at Princeton University, where he received a self-consciously discreet standing ovation.

The new liberal position on Hiss's guilt would be "case not proved," and whatever Hiss had done, what Nixon, McCarthy, and his other accusers had done was far, far worse. Sidney Hook, Hubert Humphrey, Joe Rauh, and a few others tried to keep the focus on the threat that Communist values posed to a genuinely liberal society, but it was a losing struggle. Paradoxically, McCarthy's fall undermined the intellectual foundations not of conservative anti-communism but its liberal counterpart.

From Containment to Détente

Even more paradoxical, the revelations about Stalin's tyranny in [Soviet leader Nikita] Khrushchev's secret speech in 1956 hurt the anti-Communist cause. Instead of rebuking those who defended Stalin during his bloodiest years, a chorus of young liberals and radicals argued that the speech proved that the Soviet Union had changed and that the old assumptions about Soviet ambitions and the subversive threat were obsolete. They were prepared to take Soviet claims about wanting to end the cold war and live in peace seriously. Neither the invasion of Hungary in 1956, the Berlin blockade in 1961, nor the installation of nuclear missiles on Cuba the following year could shake that confidence, since they interpreted these crises as strictly defensive moves by a Soviet Union "in transition."

In official circles, these sentiments had not yet surfaced. Instead, the end of McCarthyism marks the true beginning of what historians usually term the cold war consensus, as conservative and Taftite critiques of containment faded away and bipartisanship reigned supreme. But even there a subtle shift of emphasis was under way as the fifties wound down. Policymakers now focused on containment of the Soviet Union and red China as conventional international powers rather than as standard-bearers of an ideology.

Eisenhower, [Secretary of State John Foster] Dulles, and their diplomats dropped language about the "defeat of communism" and began talking about "peace" instead. Before the Geneva summit, Eisenhower had said he would travel anywhere, anytime, to discuss peace with the Soviet leadership (two of the key architects of this approach were McCarthy's bêtes noires, Emmett Hughes and C.D. Jackson). At the summit, he announced, "The American people want to be friends with the Soviet people. There are no natural differences between our people or our nations."

Soon talk about "peace" gave way to the desire for "peaceful coexistence." As Allen Drury was writing *Advise and Consent* in late 1958, some of the fictional senators in his novel still understood this sort of language as a pro-Soviet ploy. But in the real world, attitudes were already shifting. The traditional strategic goal of containment was now merely a short-term holding pattern, a way to force the Soviets toward the longer-term goal of coexistence—and still later of détente.

The new view among sophisticated observers was that McCarthy had revealed the ugly face of mass democracy on a scale analogous to Hitler and Mussolini.

The result was a double policy. In public, officials pushed for smooth relations with the Soviet Union, emphasizing summits, treaties, and cultural exchanges. In secret, the United States launched covert operations to contain aggression, as the new phrasing had it. The CIA, not the United Nations or NATO, became the cold war instrument of choice under Eisenhower and then under his successors. Part of this, of course, was the result of the growth of nuclear arsenals, which made open conflict with the Soviet Union unthinkable, but part of it too was a desire not to allow partisan passions to disrupt the delicate strategic balance as they had during Korea and the McCarthy era. From Iran to Guatemala (where McCarthy's old nemesis John Peurifoy helped overthrow pro-Soviet President Arbenz in 1953) to Laos, the United States began conducting a series of secret wars that the American people knew nothing about and required no prior justification among insiders and members of Congress admitted to their inner councils. In matters of foreign policy, the public was not invited.

Fear of Right-Wing Extremism

For one thing, the establishment's view of the public changed, thanks to the McCarthy episode. America, they believed, had shown itself vulnerable to a dangerous brand of radical populists who saw the world in simplistic terms and who, if allowed to enter the debate, would irrationally turn on their intellectual and social betters. The new view among sophisticated observers was that McCarthy had revealed the ugly face of mass democracy on a scale analogous to Hitler and Mussolini. Sociologists stressed the similarities between McCarthy and other American rabble-rousers like Huey Long and Father Coughlin, and Columbia's Richard Hofstadter stressed McCarthyism's "paranoid style" and the anti-intellectualism of his supporters. Professor Hofstadter even denied them the label "conservatives." They were "pseudo-conservatives" in his view, the products of "the rootlessness and heterogeneity of American life." And, he asked plaintively, "why do they express such a persistent fear and suspicion of *their* own government, whether its leadership rests in the hands of Roosevelt, Truman, or Eisenhower?" Taken together with the damning picture of McCarthy and his followers in Richard Rovere's *Senator Joe McCarthy*, which appeared in 1959, the entire period seemed to prove to liberal intellectuals that "the mass of people could not be relied on to defend civil liberties and democratic rights." America, they agreed, had just dodged a political bullet: the specter of right-wing dictatorship led by goose-stepping ranks of the American Legion and the Knights of Columbus.

Fear of right-wing extremism did not fade with McCarthy's passing. A parade of claimants to the McCarthy mantle had appeared, starting with William Jenner. After the censure, he and others worried about how to reunite the anti-Communist right. Jenner tried briefly to sustain the faithful by speaking out on the "hidden revolution" in American government that elite liberal bureaucrats were carrying out and that provided an "ideal shelter for Communists in our government," but then he too dropped off the stage. Instead, exposure of the international Communist conspiracy fell to increasingly marginal types, like John T. Flynn, Robert Welch and the John Birch Society, Willis Carlo's Liberty Lobby, John Beaty of the anti-Semitic and racist *Iron Curtain over America*, and John Stormer of *None Dare Call It Treason*. To sophisticated observers, this disparate group of men summed up the New American right, which posed a far greater danger (despite their diminutive numbers) to American freedom than a battered and discredited Communist Party.

Liberal Cold War Consensus Prevails

Any attack on liberal conduct of the cold war, insofar as it echoed "McCarthyism," automatically implied a paranoid and dysfunctional view of reality. In the cold war movie *Fail Safe*, the right-wingers all push for nuclear apocalypse (one of them, played by Walter Matthau, even looks like Mc-Carthy), while liberal president Henry Fonda and his elite private school chum, played by Dan O'Herlihy, remain calm and manage to contain the crisis by putting their faith in their Soviet counterparts—who end up looking more human and less ideological than their hard-line American opponents.

The only alternative to the liberal cold war consensus, the conventional wisdom implied, was mass destruction. At every step policymakers insisted on narrowing the range of their options, believing that America's global commitments were too vital to be handled through normal political channels or to be exploited in a "reckless" or "partisan" manner. As liberal Chester Bowles put it, Republican anti-Communist crusades had allowed "Congressional investigations and individual senators . . . to dictate day-to-day policy on foreign affairs; to make a political football of the military establishment; to punish by adverse publicity those men who were guilty of no crime punishable by law; and to divide the president from his subordinates in the Administration." The cold war required instead creative presidential leadership, with a carefully picked coterie of advisers and executive branch officials, all groomed for power and "strategic thought," the new *arcana imperii* of the nuclear age. The last thing anyone wanted were old-style "primitives" like Joe McCarthy or Kenneth Wherry wading in to insist on public debate or scrutiny, and mucking up the clean, cool dispatch of policy.

Congress by and large acquiesced. Unpleasant episodes

like the Wherry resolution, or the Bricker amendment, or McCarthy's taunting of State or Defense Department officials were past anomalies, while the Tonkin Gulf resolution became the future norm. As the sixties dawned, the new cold war ideal was of a circle of Ivy League–trained advisers sitting around a smooth, polished table with the president and coolly dealing with each crisis and Soviet move in turn, as an admiring public breathlessly waited on the results—which is precisely what the public got, first in the Cuban missile crisis and then in Vietnam. . . .

Vietnam broke the back of the liberal establishment. Stunned by their own children's revolt against the war at Harvard, Yale, Columbia, Cornell, and other elite universities; battered by the pounding waves of media criticism; and bemused by the radical restlessness of their intellectual protégés, the Best and the Brightest lost their nerve and folded. Liberal anticommunism ceased to be a viable political category. Instead, all the anti-anti-Communist propaganda of the post-McCarthy years, from Arthur Miller's *The Crucible* to Fred Cook's *Nightmare Decade* and Walter Goodman's *The Committee* (which pilloried HUAC), came home to roost. The old discredited Popular Front perspective suddenly became the conventional wisdom, and "the rigid anticommunism of the Cold War" and containment appeared as the root of all evil. Out of the resulting chaos emerged the new left, the direct biological and intellectual heirs of the "old" (that is to say, the Communist) left. Nearly every one of the architects of the Port Huron Statement, the manifesto of the new left student movement, was a child of former Communists or fellow travelers (one notable exception being Tom Hayden)—"red diaper babies," as they were called, and as they called themselves with a certain shy pride. As one of them, David Horowitz, now freely admits, "From its beginnings, the New Left was not an innocent experiment in American utopianism, but a self-conscious effort to rescue the Communist project from its Soviet fate."

The Port Huron Statement did blast "ultraconservative movements" such as the one McCarthy's heir, Barry Goldwater, was launching in the Republican Party. "It is a disgrace of the United States that such a movement should become a prominent kind of public participation in the modern world," it opined. But at the same time it welcomed the Goldwater right as a polarizing influence. Radical students hoped that it would drive the liberals out of the GOP and destabilize the bipartisan consensus that reigned over foreign and domestic policy. It was liberalism, not conservatism, that headed the new left's hit list.

The Anti-Anti-Communist Backlash

This radical shift in political mood in the academy and on the fringes of the media did not go unnoticed among those insiders who had also distrusted the old consensus. In 1966, William Fulbright published a stinging critique of America's role in the cold war, *The Arrogance of Power.* He warned that "this view of communism as an evil philosophy is a distorting prism through which we see projections of our own minds rather than what is actually there." Fulbright even conjectured, "Some countries are probably better off under communist rule. . . . Some people may even want to live under communism." For the first time since the forties, anti-anticommunism had become institutionally respectable.

At the same time, anticommunism's institutional support was fading fast. John Henry Faulk and Dalton Trumbo had broken the media blacklist years earlier. The Warren Court had pulled the teeth from most antisubversive legislation and the government's loyalty security program lapsed into desuetude. In 1950, at the height of the red scare, KGB field officers complained to their superiors about the difficulty of recruiting new agents in the "current fascist atmosphere" of a security-conscious America. Then things began to slacken. Since 1956 only four government employees and twelve applicants had been dismissed or denied employment on grounds of "reasonable doubt" regarding their loyalty to the United States. After 1968 there were none. Dismissal on security risk grounds also fell sharply. At the same time, perhaps coincidentally, there was also a steady, discernible rise in the incidence of espionage involving federal employees (particularly in the U.S. Army), culminating in the Walker family and Aldrich Ames spy cases.

In his sobering analysis of the collapse of the government's security efforts, historian Guenter Lewy is driven to conclude, "Perhaps the greatest damage that Senator Joseph McCarthy has caused this nation is that he succeeded in casting doubt upon the need for a serious and responsible concern with Communism and domestic security." Yet this argument is misleading. McCarthy was discredited and destroyed by those who claimed that his brand of anticommunism was *not* serious and responsible, while the liberal brand was: as the cliché had it, "We agree with McCarthy's aims, but not his methods." Yet very soon after overthrowing his methods, within a decade of his death, in fact, they had lost interest in the aims as well.

No one, especially in liberal circles, seemed particularly concerned by this rise in espionage cases. On the contrary, one influential liberal lobbying group after another was now admitting Communist Party members into its ranks. The civil rights movement had done so in 1964 after two decades of trying to keep Stalinists from exploiting the segregation issue for their own purposes. The next to go was SANE (the Committee for a Sane Nuclear Policy), which opened its doors to Communists in 1967, after a long and ugly fight over the issue six years earlier. The American Civil Liberties Union followed suit, although Norman Thomas pleaded with the ACLU board to keep its 1940 provision banning Communist members, arguing that "those who favor Chinese or even Russian standards of state control which make any measure of civil liberty a gift of a totalitarian government, not a right, do not belong on our governing boards." The Americans for Democratic Action's anti-Communist provisions were a dead letter by 1970. A series of articles in the *New York Times* in 1972 made Alger Hiss a new liberal hero and martyr, and HUAC fell into deep disfavor. The Senate abolished its Internal Security subcommittee in 1977, and HUAC died an unlamented death in 1975.

"Whatever else Senator McCarthy did,"
Buckley had written in 1959, *"he brought*
liberalism to a boil."

The man who had insisted on the changes at SANE, Doctor Benjamin Spock, was also an avid opponent of the Vietnam War. He and William Sloane Coffin openly urged young men to burn their draft cards, which most Americans would have labeled as incitement to treason but now drew sympathy, if not support, from the mainstream media. Spock was the most famous pediatrician in the world; Coffin was chaplain at Yale and pastor at the prestigious Riverside Church in New York. (Who now remembered J.B.

Matthews's claim that communism found some of its strongest supporters among the ranks of the Protestant clergy?) In fact, support for the Communist Vietcong among the antiwar protesters was open and unashamed. Student activists made regular trips to Hanoi and Havana to ask North Vietnamese officials how they could help them win the war. Their followers waved Vietcong flags and pictures of Ho Chi Minh at antiwar rallies, while the pacifist Fellowship for Reconciliation shipped food and supplies to North Vietnam. Peter Collier later recounted how the editorial board of the radical newspaper *Ramparts* met every Friday night to watch the CBS evening news and stand up and cheer when Walter Cronkite read the weekly death toll of Americans killed in Vietnam.

It was the nightmare McCarthy and Jenner had conjured up more [than] a decade earlier, of American liberals and radicals allying themselves with domestic Communists on one side and with foreign totalitarians on the other. But in 1968 no one dared to say a word; that would have smacked of McCarthyism. . . .

Bringing Liberalism to a Boil

By 1960 McCarthy's old ally and friend Barry Goldwater had assumed the role as spokesman for a wholesale rejection of "modern" Republicanism, symbolized by Nelson Rockefeller. That year Brent Bozell ghost-wrote Goldwater's manifesto, *The Conscience of a Conservative*, which became an instant best-seller. The book heralded the reemergence of a political movement that owed its ideology to Robert Taft but found a much broader social and geographic base, running from the traditionally Democratic South to the West and the American heartland. By 1968 a farsighted political analyst named Kevin Phillips was already dubbing this "Southern, Western—and Irish—backed" antiestablishmentarian movement the New Republican Majority.

The truth was that it was not ordinary middle-class and working-class Americans who had been terrorized by McCarthy and the red scare, but the liberals and the intellectuals. "Whatever else Senator McCarthy did," Buckley had written in 1959, "he brought liberalism to a boil." It was they, even more than the Communists, who perceived him as a threat. In trying to undo his political legacy, they in fact unraveled themselves. Liberals used the specter of Mc-

Carthyism as a stick with which to beat back this conservative insurgency. That tactic worked in 1964 as Goldwater went down to a humiliating defeat. But below the waterline the movement had stuck fast, an increasingly heavy barnacle on the ship of state despite every attempt to scrape it off.

It may be true, as Michael Paul Rogin and others have claimed, that McCarthy failed to set off a populist revolt. But his ideological heirs did. When Ronald Reagan assumed the leadership of a reconstituted conservative GOP in 1980, it had a distinctly populist appeal. It was Republicans, not Democrats, who could now claim to represent "ordinary working Americans," while liberalism slid deeper and deeper into division and self-doubt.

In the end, then, McCarthy was always a more important figure to American liberals than to conservatives. The nightmarish image of his heavy, swarthy, sweaty features haunted the imaginations of thousands of anti-anti-Communists throughout the sixties and seventies. It appeared and reappeared in documentaries like *Point of Order* and *Seeing Red* and helped to set off the backlash that brought liberal anticommunism crashing to the floor.

Important Figures
of the McCarthy Era

Dean Acheson: President Truman's secretary of state from 1949 to 1953. McCarthy accused Acheson of protecting Communists in the State Department. During McCarthy's hearings on subversive activities, Acheson stated that he would not fire any State Department subordinates.

John Adams: An army counsel. The Senate committee that investigated McCarthy found that Adams had "made efforts to terminate or influence the investigation and hearings at Fort Monmouth." Fort Monmouth is an army facility that McCarthy claimed was the base for a spy ring set up by Julius Rosenberg, who had been executed for spying in 1953.

Alexander Barmine: A former brigadier general in the Soviet army who defected from the Soviet Union in 1937. He testified at the Army-McCarthy hearings.

Earl Browder: General secretary of the Communist Party of the United States of America from 1929 to 1944. A faked photo of Browder with Senator Millard Tydings led to Tydings's defeat in the 1950 elections.

Louis Budenz: During the early 1940s, managing editor of the Communist newspaper the *Daily Worker* and a member of the Communist Party's national committee. He eventually renounced communism and returned to the Catholic Church. In April 1950, Budenz testified before the Senate Foreign Relations Committee that State Department adviser Owen Lattimore belonged to a Communist cell.

Roy M. Cohn: Appointed by McCarthy in 1953 as chief counsel to the Senate's Permanent Investigations Subcommittee. When Cohn's closest friend, G. David Schine, was drafted into the army in November of that year, Cohn and McCarthy failed to win him a commission. Their failure led to the two mens declaring a war on the army, which eventually resulted in the Army-McCarthy hearings.

Henry C. Dworshak: A Republican senator from Minnesota and a staunch ally of McCarthy. He replaced McCarthy as chairman of the Senate Permanent Investigations Subcommittee when he stepped down during the Army-McCarthy hearings. The subcommittee would find McCarthy innocent of trying to exert personal pressure on the army in the Schine imbroglio. Dworshak was also one of only twenty-two senators who voted against censuring McCarthy.

Frederick Fisher: A lawyer who belonged to army counsel Joseph Welch's law firm. During the hearings, McCarthy repeatedly pestered Joseph Welch, special counsel for the army, about Fisher and his associations, including his former membership in the National Lawyers Guild. Guild members represented the Rosenbergs and the Hollywood Ten, among others, during the McCarthy era.

Ralph E. Flanders: A Republican senator from Vermont. In July 1954, disturbed by McCarthy's reckless claims about Communist infiltration of the U.S. government and military, Flanders introduced a resolution to censure the Wisconsin senator. The Senate approved the resolution on December 2, 1954, by a 67-22 vote.

Haldore Hanson: A State Department administrator who, according to testimony by Louis Budenz, was a member of the Communist Party. When McCarthy spoke before the Tydings Committee, he stated his concerns about Hanson's power to distribute foreign aid.

Reed Harris: A high-ranking State Department official who challenged McCarthy's actions. In a 1953 hearing on whether Communists were infiltrating Voice of America, McCarthy accused Harris of being a Communist. McCarthy cited a book Harris had written in the 1930s, *King Football*, as proof, because Harris had written in favor of full academic teaching rights for Communists. Harris denied the allegations.

H. Struve Hensel: Assistant defense secretary and general counsel for the Defense Department from 1953 to 1954. McCarthy accused Hensel during the hearings of selling goods illegally to the U.S. Navy during World War II. Mc-Carthy later admitted his charges were false.

Bourke Hickenlooper: A Republican senator from Iowa who served on the Tydings Committee that investigated McCarthy's allegations of Communists in the State Department. He did not sign the committee's report that cleared the State Department and chastised McCarthy, nor did he vote in favor of censure of McCarthy in 1954.

Alger Hiss: A former State Department official who was indicted for giving classified documents to Whittaker Chambers, an admitted Communist, in 1948. Hiss was convicted two years later. His conviction helped set the stage for the rise of McCarthy.

J. Edgar Hoover: FBI director from 1935 until 1972. A McCarthy ally, he was heavily involved in the Alger Hiss investigation and helped uncover the spy ring of Julius and Ethel Rosenberg, Klaus Fuchs, and Harry Gold.

Henry Jackson: A Democratic senator from Washington who strongly disliked McCarthy and his methods. His questions at the Army-McCarthy hearings helped lead to Mc-Carthy's censure.

Owen Lattimore: A professor at Johns Hopkins University and a scholar on China who was targeted by the anti-Communist lobby for his association with left-wing organizations and alleged sympathy for the Soviet Union. In 1949, Alexander Barmine named Lattimore a Soviet agent, a remark reiterated by McCarthy the following year.

George Marshall: Five-star general of the army and statesman best known for his plan to rebuild Europe's economy after World War II. McCarthy falsely claimed that Marshall was a leader of a pro-Communist conspiracy that also included President Truman and Dean Acheson.

Harvey Matusow: An FBI informant on Communist Party activities in New York. At the Army-McCarthy hearings, he testified about the spread of communism in the U.S. government. He would later recant his testimony.

Pat McCarran: A Democratic senator from Nevada who chaired the Senate Internal Security Committee and was known for his staunch anti-Communist views and his alliance with fellow senators McCarthy and William E. Jenner. He led the passage of the McCarran-Wood Act in 1950, which required Communist organizations to register with the U.S. attorney general and placed travel and employment restrictions on known Communists.

John L. McClellan: A Democratic senator from Arkansas. In 1953 he led a Democratic boycott of the Permanent Investigations Subcommittee headed by McCarthy, charging that McCarthy treated the committee like a one-man show.

Miles Reber: Commanding general of the U.S. Army in Europe when he testified at the Army-McCarthy hearings. Reber testified that McCarthy and Cohn had tried to pressure him into obtaining a commission for G. David Schine.

Samuel Reber: Miles Reber's brother and the acting high commissioner for the State Department in Germany when Cohn and G. David Schine had toured Europe in order to determine whether American officials living overseas were aware of the Communist threat. During the Army-McCarthy hearings, McCarthy wrongly accused Reber of hiring a man to follow Cohn and Schine throughout Europe. McCarthy's associates also threatened to make public a homosexual relationship Reber had as an undergraduate. Reber would eventually resign from the State Department.

G. David Schine: Roy Cohn's closest friend. Cohn and McCarthy's unsuccessful efforts to get Schine a commission in the army led to the Army-McCarthy hearings.

Stuart Symington: A Democratic senator from Missouri. He was a member of the committee that conducted the Army-McCarthy hearings and was McCarthy's most vocal antagonist.

Millard Tydings: A Democratic senator from Maryland. In 1950, Tydings was named the chair of a special Senate committee to investigate McCarthy's allegations that Communists in the State Department were significantly influencing America's foreign policy. The Tydings Committee found all of McCarthy's claims false. Tydings lost the 1950 election when a faked photograph showing him conversing with former Communist Party leader Earl Browder was distributed.

Edmund Walsh: A prominent Roman Catholic priest and one of McCarthy's closest advisers. In May 1950, he suggested that McCarthy—who was concerned about that fall's elections—begin a campaign against Communist subversives working in the Truman administration.

Joseph Welch: Special counsel for the army during the Army-McCarthy hearings. His condemnation of McCarthy during the senator's questioning of Frederick Fisher helped turn public opinion against McCarthy.

For Further Research

Dean Acheson, *Present at the Creation: My Years in the State Department*. New York: W.W. Norton, 1969.

William F. Buckley Jr. and L. Brent Bozell, *McCarthy and His Enemies: The Record and Its Meaning*. Washington, DC: Regnery, 1954.

David Caute, *The Great Fear: The Anti-Communist Purge Under Truman and Eisenhower*. New York: Simon and Schuster, 1978.

Roy Cohn, *McCarthy*. New York: New American Library, 1968.

Griffin Fariello, *Red Scare: Memories of the American Inquisition: An Oral History*. New York: W.W. Norton, 1995.

Richard Freeland, *The Truman Doctrine and the Origins of McCarthyism: Foreign Policy, Domestic Politics, and Internal Security, 1946–1948*. New York: Alfred A. Knopf, 1972.

Robert Griffith, *The Politics of Fear: Joseph R. McCarthy and the Senate*. Amherst: University of Massachusetts Press, 1970.

M.J. Heale, *McCarthy's Americans: Red Scare Politics in State and Nation, 1935–1965*. Athens: University of Georgia Press, 1998.

Arthur Herman, *Joseph McCarthy: Reexamining the Life and Legacy of America's Most Hated Senator*. New York: Free Press, 2000.

Mark Landis, *Joseph McCarthy: The Politics of Chaos*. Selinsgrove, PA: Susquehanna University Press, 1987.

Earl Latham, ed., *The Meaning of McCarthyism*. Lexington, MA: D.C. Heath, 1973.

Sidney Lens, *The Futile Crusade: Anti-Communism as American Credo*. Chicago: Quadrangle Books, 1964.

Allan J. Matusow, *Joseph R. McCarthy*. Englewood Cliffs, NJ: Prentice-Hall, 1970.

Joseph R. McCarthy, *McCarthyism: The Fight for America, Documented Answers to Questions Asked by Friend and Foe*. New York: Devin-Adair, 1952.

Douglas T. Miller and Marion Nowak, *The Fifties: The Way We Really Were*. Garden City, NY: Doubleday, 1975.

David M. Oshinsky, *A Conspiracy So Immense: The World of Joe McCarthy*. New York: Free Press, 1983.

Charles E. Potter, *Days of Shame*. New York: Coward-McCann, 1965.

Thomas C. Reeves, *The Life and Times of Joe McCarthy*. New York: Stein and Day, 1982.

Thomas C. Reeves, ed., *McCarthyism*. Hinsdale, IL: Dryden Press, 1973.

Richard H. Rovere, *Senator Joe McCarthy*. New York: Harcourt, Brace, Jovanovich, 1959.

Ellen Schrecker, *Many Are the Crimes, McCarthyism in America*. Boston: Little, Brown, 1998.

I.F. Stone, *The Haunted Fifties*. New York: Random House, 1969.

Michael Straight, *Trial by Television*. Boston: Beacon Press, 1954.

Athan Theoharis, ed., *From the Secret Files of J. Edgar Hoover*. Chicago: Ivan R. Dee, 1991.

Index